HUMAN PSYCHE
IN
PSYCHOANALYSIS

The Development of Three Models
of Psychoanalytic Therapy

By

BENJAMIN WOLSTEIN, Ph.D.

Faculty, W. A. White Institute of Psychiatry, Psychoanalysis andPsychology
New York, New York
Clinical Professor Psychology, Adelphi University
Garden City, New York

CHARLES C THOMAS • PUBLISHER
Springfield • Illinois • U.S.A.

Published and Distributed Throughout the World by
CHARLES C THOMAS • PUBLISHER
Bannerstone House
301-327 East Lawrence Avenue, Springfield, Illinois, U.S.A.
Natchez Plantation House
735 North Atlantic Boulevard, Fort Lauderdale, Florida, U.S.A.

With *THOMAS BOOKS careful attention is given to all details of
manufacturing and design. It is the Publisher's desire to present books that are
satisfactory as to their physical qualities and artistic possibilities and
appropriate for their particular use. THOMAS BOOKS will be true to those
laws of quality that assure a good name and good will.*

Printed in the United States of America
RN-1

This Book Is Dedicated

To the Memory of My Teacher,
CLARA THOMPSON,
Who Believed Psychoanalysis Is Science

and

My Mother,
REBECCA WOLSTEIN,
Who Believed the Torah of Her Pure Spirit

PREFACE

INDIVIDUALITY requires the endeavor of human psyche to persist as it is and become what it can. It requires a personal sense of making psychic resources into beliefs, values and ideals, of completing the psychic endowment of feeling, thinking and acting. But the important point is that only in psychological terms can it be properly understood. In biological terms, the individual psyche would mean adjustment of oral, anal, genital and other bodily zones to their respective environments; in short, id and need satisfaction. In sociological terms, it would point up adaptation to established patterns of relatedness and communication; in short, ego defense and interpersonal security. To be anything at all in psychoanalysis, individuality and self-direction must then be viewed as affective and cognitive to the limits of psychic endowment and capable of being worked through the growing edge of shared experience.

This development of psychic function needs no justification for its undertaking other than being there to be developed. Based in human strivings for knowledge and truth, insight and fulfillment, it antecedes the use of psychology to defend biological pleasure and secure ego-interpersonal power. For the very essence of human psyche is, I believe, this curiosity, this desire to know in the widest sense, without which, no doubt, the psychoanalytic enterprise itself could never have been brought into being.

CONTENTS

HUMAN PSYCHE
IN
PSYCHOANALYSIS

The Development of Three Models
of Psychoanalytic Therapy

Other Books by Benjamin Wolstein

Theory of Psychoanalytic Therapy
Freedom to Experience
Irrational Despair
Countertransference
Transference
Experience and Valuation

Chapter 1

THE BIOLOGICAL MODEL

As historical background for development of the psychological model of psychoanalysis, it is necessary to review some procedures of the biological and sociological models designed to manipulate the patient in therapy. Lengthy statements and criticisms of both these models already exist in the literature, and I do not reproduce them here. Students of psychoanalysis are undoubtedly acquainted with the original and secondary sources, while the uninitiated reader desiring further study may consider books and papers noted in the following chapters, as well as the bibliographies to which they, in turn, refer. In Chapter 1 and Chapter 3, the historical sketches are therefore limited to the above purpose.

Starting with the biological model, it is not difficult to show that the first psychoanalysis of transference is manipulative. Its roots as definition and procedure trace back to hypnosis and cathartic therapy. But in order to avoid distortion, neither the definition nor the procedure may be reduced to any such previous context of therapeutic inquiry.* The fact that a definition is stated and a procedure applied for authoritarian purposes, for example, differs from the fact that their metapsychology reaches beyond psychotherapy into widely accepted philosophies such as biological and social Darwinism. It also differs from the view that nineteenth-century monarchical beliefs, values and ideals filtered through the intellectual climate in which psychoanalysis originated and became solidified in the biological model.

There is real difference between empirical observation and systematic explanation on one side, and the social and cultural environs for which they are interpreted on the other. This

---

*See Freud, S.: *A General Introduction to Psychoanalysis.* Garden City, Garden City, 1943, especially Chapter 27 and Chapter 28; and his Papers on technique, In *Collected Papers,* London, Hogarth, 1924, vol. 2, pp. 305-402.

difference is built into psychoanalysis as the fundamental distinction of psychology from metapsychology — a distinction that keeps various levels of inquiry from obstructing, or even overrunning, one another. Perhaps negligible from the point of view of gross pragmatism, this distinction, in turn, makes all the difference in any psychotherapy between a closed system of doctrine and freedom of creative discovery. Especially in psychoanalytic therapy is this clear. Compare the patient who formally enacts patterns already in existence with one who makes his individual and emergent. As long as imaginative intelligence continues to generate visions that bump into the walls of established doctrine, this comparison will remain relevant to all psychotherapy.

In the biological model, psychoanalysis of transference is a procedure of managing the patient's relation to his problems. The patient as person is not, of course, identical with his problems, and no psychoanalyst who uses this model would equate the two. As abstract commitment, he actually regards self-determination very highly; he obviously presupposes it in various contexts of his therapeutic inquiry. But this not the point. It is, rather, that his described procedure treats the patient's problems as though they were foreign bodies to be checked and cured by intervening psychotherapeutic antibodies, as though they were discrete entities whose libido he releases before returning them, now reinterpreted, to the patient's own active direction. His interpretation follows a theory of instinct or id impulse whose basic lines may always be modified and extended to fit any particular case without, of course, ever being so modified as to extend beyond this biological metapsychology itself.

In the experiential field of therapy, the id psychoanalyst proposes to replace his patient's active powers of resolving problems under inquiry with his own. To this end, he substitutes his own ego and superego for his patient's and proceeds to psychoanalyze his patient's id in order to resolve his id problems. He assumes their roots to be so buried in unconscious experience that only after interpretation reconstitutes their original happening can a patient freely change. But which interpretation? And who makes it? To give the obvious answers to these questions would no doubt grossly oversimply statements of the actualities of id therapy. The dominant interpretive metapsychology belongs to the id psychoanalyst whenever he offers a patient his therapeutic services. But this alone does not suffice to account for the two coparticipants maintaining their special field of inquiry and experience over long months and years. If it were merely a question of his interpretation being the more illuminating, after a thorough exchange of opinions and airing of differences and effort at persuasion, they could simply part company.

It is instructive here to recall that Freud reports obtaining his best results with patients who relate to him through child-parent images and transfer libidinal love. Left open to conjecture — a reader's and presumably also a patient's — is his experience of countertransference. In the practice of id therapy, he recommends evenly distributed attitudes of attention to a patient's relatedness and communication. But the above conjecture, as further evidence for the universal scope of id metapsychology, suggests that his best results depend on his relating from the other side through parent-child images and countertransferring libidinal love. If an id psychoanalyst does not consider countertransference instinctual, why exclude it from the experiential field of therapy altogether? But how, in the biological model, could he interpret it otherwise?

After this blackout of countertransference, the distance from libidinizing parent-child images with patients to exercising authoritarian attitudes toward them is not great. When travelled within the fixed boundaries of a universal biological metapsychology, it becomes even shorter. To make his procedure workable, the id psychoanalyst does not probe or explore initially positive transference but instead, uses it both as ground for having the patients associate to their problems and as support for interpreting their unconscious dimensions instinctually. However positive transference actually unfolds, he puts special emphasis on its persuasive support for his interpretations. Even a cursory reading of Freud's clinical studies points up this view.

Since the patient, being adult, undergoes positive transference against a self-directive background of experience, its manifestations can only be superficial. When a patient invites the id psychoanalyst to solve the riddle of his problems, and if the psychoanalyst, in turn, believes its interpretation requires a parent-child psychodrama, no deeply troubled yet cooperative adult can do less than produce it. In effect, he indicates, "I cannot understand my problems on my own, so I'll help the id psychoanalyst see what he can do about them." If he, in this circumstance, fails to manifest the positive transference of parent-child psychodrama, he is diagnosed as suffering from narcissism and therefore unpsychoanalyzable. Curiously enough, the diagnosis has a certain inner thread of logic. If the patient consults an id psychoanalyst who requires the development of such transference, he has to be practically psychotic not to attempt it; or if he truly cannot develop it, at least appear to do so. Genuine or simulated, the initially positive transference, however, manifests only transitory patterns of dependency of a patient in deeper psychological trouble.

The id patient, it may now be clear, cooperates in producing parental images of his childhood for his therapist's procedure, and no therapist's psychic powers could create them unaided. He does so by voluntarily, and indeed willfully, relaxing adult standards of common sense, practical reason and social intelligence. During id therapy, psychosexual interpretation stands up far better for the child's unfettered imagination, moreover, than to the adult's critical thought. Intrinsic merits of this type of interpretation aside, however, dramatic changes in the interpersonal relations of psychoanalyst and patient are inevitable after early amenities of positive transference wear thin and eventually wear off. Only when positive transference turns negative and resistive and the patient no longer easily assents to his psychoanalyst's interpretations is it judged worthy of serious inquiry. But this is like locking the barn after the horse escapes, for the patient has already accommodated his id psychoanalyst, worked himself into the required childlike relationship and lived through tutorial experience as a result of moving his own adult psychology away from the center of the therapeutic field. Deciding to study transference now, and not while it was initially positive, the id psychoanalyst underlines a special instance of arbitrariness about clinical matters.

To this point, id therapy may be characterized as arising from the psychoanalyst's positive countertransference to his patient's transference. Recalling the early and strong dissatisfaction with hypnosis and cathartic therapy, it may be inferred that this positive countertransference is, however, also superficial. And may it accordingly be hypothesized that as transference becomes negative, so does countertransference? The answer is difficult to make out for the reason that therapeutic inquiry would probably terminate before such an eventuality fully developed, since it made no clear provision for working through initially negative transference.

The id psychoanalyst works best with varieties of hysteria from the anxious to the borderline that manifest varieties of transference of love. To its negative qualities, it is clear here, he responds negatively. Before they openly emerge, he negates them by simply ignoring the evidence for them. And when they do emerge in full, he undertakes with his patient to negate them — to overcome, to conquer them as resistance to his interpretive metapsychology. Despite long and intensive therapy of these patients, he finally concludes that he does not, interestingly enough, know what a woman really wants. As though this were not itself a worthy problem for future psychoanalytic inquiry, he also concludes that the great riddle of feminine psychology, in fact, belongs to biology. After the relevant psychological processes and patterns are adequately interpreted from a biological point of view, the inquiry comes to an end and therapy may be terminated. But if the psychoanalytic problem of women, in truth, belongs to biology, no psychology can ever hope to solve anything about feminine experience. For if it is true that the terms of feminine psychology are to be sought and found in biology, how do those of masculine psychology escape being also sought and found in biology? And if, going to the logical end, these inquiries belong to biology, why attempt psychological analysis of them altogether? Why introduce psychological means at all? Instead, why not go straight to biology?

It is no news that psychoanalysts have a venerated traditions of rushing into problems where the angels fear to tread. That Freud finally valued the search for imaginative vision far above the research of empirical generalizations in large measure accounts for his lasting charisma in this field. For this reason, there is the staying power of his work, which still symbolizes devotion to intensive study of that vast unconscious reservoir of unknown and unrealized potentialities of the distinctly human in experience. The power of his symbolic value is not diminished by the fact that he wrongly set biology as the future direction of the study of human psyche. Such lapses, so far, do not detract from the charisma of his image of seeking truth all the way. For though finally baffled by the psychology of both men and women and then finding scientific respite in biology, he certainly made it possible for later psychoanalysts to be far more courageous — feeling far less foolish, as well, without having to be angels either — about undertaking adventures into the psychological unknown.

The major problem of id metapsychology, of course, is still the basic nature of psychological differences between men and women. Seen and treated in biological terms since the beginning of psychoanalysis, the problem remains unanswered to this day. The possibility has to be faced now that it cannot be answered in the original terms of id metapsychology. And if psychological means are somehow expected to explore and explain biological factors, the probability also has to be faced now that it will remain unanswered. Perhaps the more fruitful avenue is the less traditional one of looking directly at psychological differentia among human beings in their individuality — without, in principle, overemphasizing sexual and other biological differentia — and then focusing on processes and patterns of human psyche that a psychoanalytic inquiry may best explore and explain.

In order to appreciate why the id psychoanalyst manipulates his patient's therapeutic experience, it is also necessary to recall another critical but neglected piece of history. It cannot be cited too often because no practicing id psychoanalyst should forget it; Freud never did. The biological model is explicitly designed to achieve, unchanged in psychoanalysis, the earlier and well-established goals of hypnosis and cathartic therapy — "descriptively, to recover lost memories and, dynamically, to conquer resistances caused by repression."* Since with Breuer, his teacher,

*Freud, S.: Further recommendations in the technique of psychoanalysis. In *Collected Papers*. London, Hogarth, 1924, vol. 2, p. 367.

he first set them in their 1893-1895 *Studies on Hysteria,* through all later theory and practice he never discarded them. In psychoanalysis, he changed only the means to achieve and meanings to interpret them; but the goals themselves remained the same.

The chief strength of this biological model, however, was to become its chief weakness. Its psychological value derives from the profoundly hypnotic and cathartic talking cure that Breuer first hit upon with Anna O. This is its chief strength. But pursuing the two goals of this therapy, as stated above, Freud gradually narrowed down the actual range of his empirical and systematic inquiry to subject matter that best supports them in psycho-analysis — which, of course, would also serve as a valid design for Breuer's clinical field of inquiry. This is its chief weakness. He did not rework and restate these goals, even after moving his therapeutic inquiry into fields of experience that fundamentally differ from those of hypnosis and cathartic therapy. Nor, indeed, did he rework and restate them in response to the more profound and unprecedented goals and perspectives made visible on these new psychological horizons of psychoanalytic inquiry and experience.

A psychoanalytic psychology fully appropriate to its empirical and systematic subject matter is still not complete and fully coordinated. It is not my intent, obviously, to suggest that Freud should have outlined the structure of psychoanalysis in more contemporary directions. It is, rather, to consider what he actually did as a result of narrowing the goals of psychoanalysis to those of hypnosis. Following leads to recovery of lost oedipal memories and deliberately proceeding to overcome resistances to their recall, he designed a very special type of psychogenetic inquiry.

His effort to ground such eminently psychological processes as memory and recall in a biological metapsychology is, however, an unenviable theoretical task on its face. Throughout, it carries the extremely difficult burden of fusing biology with psychology — two fields of inquiry, of course, still very distinct in procedure and result — and confusing psychological conditions of hypnosis with those of psychoanalysis in order to make interpretations accord with the biological model. But look briefly at the improbable paradox of this effort. Despite Freud's practice of a psychological inquiry no longer hypnotic in procedure, despite his separation in psychological terms of hypnotic goals from hypnotic procedures and despite his later pursuit of these same goals in other procedures, he had a hard faith in the promise of biology to interpret the performance of psychoanalysis. In order to accord unconscious psychology with id metapsychology, that is, he continued to seek the goals of hypnosis without modification or enlargement; and the two sides of his thought never did meet.

It is in terms of this paradox rather than personality or culture that I propose that Freud did not recognize and directly treat transference of love as the self-distortion it patently and openly is. He did not, because even if distorted, such positive qualities are good temporary supports for recovering lost oedipal memories and overcoming resistances to their recall — the two goals of hypnosis first extended into cathartic therapy, then into the pressure procedure and, with id interpretation added, finally into psychoanalytic therapy. So much for direct statement of the answer; I now consider some reasons why it is probably the best one.

As long as a patient has memories and associations suitable for interpretation, the id psychoanalyst's standard procedure is to leave transference of love alone, no matter how distorted its qualities and directions. He is far more concerned about applying the postulates of genesis and dynamism than any of the others, and this is the rationale of his procedure. A significant part of psychoanalytic inquiry to this day is to trace back processes and patterns of transference to their familial origins. It is still useful to explore these psychological origins in relation to later increments of change, both inside and outside the family. Taking the genetic point of view, the id psychoanalyst and his patient attempt to transform current transference into memories of actual and imagined history, obtaining information about earlier sources of transference chosen for study. In this genetic view, they may then delineate the rise of processes and the development of their patterns in various fields of past experience through various stages of personality evolving. But equally important for the future of their working inquiry, they discover whether the psychoanalyst is aware enough to make, and the patient open enough to take, id interpretations of this newly integrated field of experience.

Interest in genesis has as long a history in psychoanalysis as psychoanalysis itself. From the very beginning, early childhood experience has accordingly been emphasized in the extreme. In the service of this end, it is necessary to turn aside from current functions of psychological process or pattern in favor of the past history of their contents. In order to seek this end, it is, however, also necessary to believe that uncovering such history is far more important than discovering why a patient, here and now, distorts love in the unconscious present of psychoanalytic experience. Exploring the actual and current field in which a patient transfers love to a psychoanalyst is not considered as relevant, either. In procedures of id therapy, a psychoanalyst undertakes this sort of exploration essentially to extend the genetic postulate over most of the working inquiry. He uniformly relates the contents of transference to memories of actual or imagined history and, in so doing, adds his support to the wisdom of common sense that knowing history is the best safeguard against repeating it. But in human psychology, this unfortunately does not check out. A knowledge of history does not ordinarily release this power to change. Such knowledge, it is true, provides some conditions for change; but it does not by itself empower its possessor to act otherwise. For knowledge obtained by genetic analysis, like that obtained by using the other postulates, needs that special leaven of insight and choice to free the individual's psyche for self-direction.

This special use of genesis in the biological model differs from its use in later models, and this is the essential point for future inquiry. The id psychoanalyst does not treat the substance of distortion as though its transformation were the primary reason for the whole inquiry. Instead, he treats it as providing materials for a postdictive delineation of the past. Perhaps because of the thick nineteenth-century romance with history and evolution — distant origins, early genesis, deep roots — he believes it more important to penetrate memories of, for example, the third or fourth year in childhood than to study actual and current transference of distortion in therapy. And the id psychoanalyst does this indirectly, all the while assuming that transformation of ongoing process or pattern into actual or imagined history makes it unnecessary afterward to confront the transferred distortion as well; it is somehow supposed to change automatically. But observe here that he also expects the adult ego or interpersonal self, after obtaining the rightly interpreted genetic information, to be able to modify it straightaway.

Unlike those practicing the sociological model considered in Chapter 3, the id psychoanalyst does not explicitly attempt to explore, clarify and reconstruct patterns of the ego or interpersonal self. He does not work directly with transference of ego defense or interpersonal security operation. Id patients are not pixilated, persnikety or pig-headed; they are open, cooperative and sweet-smiling. The psychoanalyst does not, moreover, use the genetic postulate with actual transferred distortion for the therapeutic purpose of obtaining clearer awareness of their live process and pattern here and now. As a result, genesis tends to pervade his field of inquiry to the point of substituting historicogenetic study of childhood experience for the primary objective of the whole inquiry — that is, psychological change.

Other postulates or points of view in the biological model are dynamism, structure, topography, economy. But since genesis is most amenable to both the empirical and the interpretive operations through various phases of therapeutic inquiry, it lends itself best to id psychoanalysis of transference of love. They have all, of course, been modified and restated over the years, yet none, it is fair to say, ever became as prominent in procedure as genesis — not even the dynamic view, the main interpretive point of this biological model. This is so, I think, because genesis meets the general requirements of empirical inquiry while, as first stated, the other four peculiarly suit the interpretive slant of id metapsychology. Without them it is not possible; without it, they are not necessary.

Chapter 2

QUESTIONS ABOUT ID THERAPY

IN the practice of any model of psychoanalytic therapy, it requires tact, skill and alertness to prevent the historical and genetic emphasis from overflowing the field of inquiry. This is so not only because of traditional usage in the biological model but also because of misguided expectations of serious though naive patients who hear that childhood history is the royal road to psychological change. Other postulates as well may be used to extend the empirical range of observation and definition in support of beliefs, values and ideals that inspire the visions of various other metapsychologies. Table I in Appendix A is arranged to illustrate this. Toward this end, (3) postulation may be so stated as to coordinate (1) observation and (2) definition with explanatory (4) theory without, however, establishing any single (5) metapsychology as absolute or exclusive in psycho-analysis.

For the present discussion, it suffices to indicate how postulating function as a complement of genesis is a counter-balance to the one-sided id inquiry into transference. Recall the suggestion made in·Chapter 1 about aspects of distortion being lived through the unconscious present. This obviously is not a historical issue in its own terms. It cannot, therefore, be directly answered by genetic exploration — no more than digging at the roots of a grapevine reveals how grapes turn into wine or later, why the wine may turn sour. Many complex patterns of relatedness and communication, organized as personal psychology, intervene between a hypothesized childhood trauma and observable distortions in the experiential field of therapy. As transferred, these psychological patterns do not appear in pure form for test-tube study under laboratory conditions.

The same may also be said about such other definitions as resistance, anxiety, counteranxiety, counterresistance and countertransference. But the emphasis here is on transference, the major defined focus of id therapy. Its manifestations do not appear in pure form because the patient always relates them at a particular time and place to a particular psychoanalyst who relates his own countertransference through a particular phase of their inquiry and experience. Like assessing the wine that turns sour, it is possible to treat distortions of transference only as they actually appear and not before their emergence in relatedness and communication. There is, moreover, no point to treating them as superficial and irrelevant and as if through a countertransferred compulsion to repeat, then looking for their id origins in early childhood automatically. Or in the wine analogy, there is no point to seeking the origins of sour wine in how grapes grow or, even earlier, in when and where vines are planted. Clearly, this is no way to learn how distortions of transference are now manifested in relation to the psychoanalyst receiving them.

Transformation of transference observed and defined in unconscious present experience is the objective of function. By this postulate, it is often found that the patient distorts the ongoing context of communication with her psychoanalyst — to pick up again the thread of feminine psychology — because she has come to believe that if she tells it straight out, she will no longer be able to attain her real psychological objective. This, of course, is genuine individuality, the crux of her therapeutic problem. In terms of it, she distorts herself and deceives her psychoanalyst, still hoping to be understood. Such hope has most probably been frustrated in distortion and deception through countless previous fields of her life experience. But painful and disfigured though it may become, even frustrated hope is still better than no hope at all. For in a vital sense, it sustains that thin thread of sanity now so deeply internalized that it can no longer unravel as clear awareness with its full significance in the open. If a skilled and careful psychoanalyst does not attend to this inner sense of continuity under the special conditions of psychotherapeutic inquiry, it is not likely that anyone else will ever do so in the ordinary situations of everyday life.

Before interpreting metapsychology or even indicating unconscious possibilities, the psychoanalyst may study this patient's relations to him in great detail. The postulate of function governs such study by, for example, comparing responses she expects with those she elicits from him. This occurs because he, and no other, happens to be her psychoanalyst in that inquiry and experience. But is this not, in fact, the regular procedure of choice? It is not the id psychoanalyst's; he chooses not to follow it. Working backward rather than forward, he studies the functional vicissitudes, instead, looking for interpretable clues to early experience. The reason he does not work the other way around is that the biological model requires him to locate individual origins of neurosis in her libidinal attachments to parents and other influential adults of her childhood. This, incidentally, is the kernel of Freud's criticism of Bernheim, namely that this outstanding nineteenth-century hypnotist did not understand the nature of trance or the later recall of hypnotic suggestion because he had no libido theory.

The biological model, however, has no postulate of function. Or as Freud might have put it, it has no functional point of view. Rather, id therapy focuses mainly on genesis in the hard belief that this postulate eventually yields supporting evidence for the libido theory. It is also because of genesis that Sullivan — without libido theory, of course — pushes interpersonal therapy back into dimly remembered discriminations of good and bad mother in the early verbal and parataxic mode and beyond that into that preverbal and prototaxic mode in which the infant first catches its mother's euphoria and anxiety through contagion. And it is difficult to overlook how Rank, searching for the individual origins of trauma, pushes genesis as far back as the birth experience itself. But it is Freud and his teachers in hypnosis, cathartic therapy and psychopathology (Bernheim, Breuer and Charcot) who establish the appeal to the genetic postulate as dominant for the first and later models of psychoanalysis.

Together with genesis, a postulate such as function, however, helps to clear the therapeutic field of premature explanation and interpretation. For it is still not known beyond doubt that every patient's problems are, of course, entirely rooted in early childhood experience. Some psychoanalysts who fully appreciate the ineradicability of this gap in clinical knowledge still do not fully break with the genetic bias of id therapy. They continue to take detailed histories with great critical care as though they were following unquestionable truth, not an arbitrary postulate. Meanwhile, here and now, they are tacitly collecting cues and clues to ego or interpersonal self presented in the experiential field of therapy. But the difference between what they say and what they do still exists, and in order to bridge it, genesis is specifically paired with function in statements of psychoanalytic procedure. I consider this theme further in Chapter 11.

Not only does function correct for the one-sided concern with genetic materials and clear the therapeutic field of premature interpretive work; it also slants inquiry into transference of love in a new direction. This point has special relevance to the present discussion, indicating that it is no longer necessary to treat transference of love simply and solely as a current facsimile of early childhood experience. Disregard here the possibility that the patient's love may be genuine. Regardless of its psychoanalyzable effects on therapeutic inquiry, it is not, as such, psychoanalyzable. Consider instead that it is distorted, so that function treats it as now reflecting the patterns of compliance and dependency she still assimilates from standard yet distorted attitudes of her family, ongoing or recalled, that she has never stopped to appraise on, or as her own.

It therefore becomes important for her therapy that she is able to determine whose attitudes she now possesses in readiness for transference of love to her psychoanalyst during certain phases of their working inquiry. In order to do so, she has to learn the critical difference − for perhaps the first time − between attitudes toward and attitudes of the significant adults of her childhood. This is so if she loves them − obviously an attitude toward − and if, to manifest it while growing up, she assimilates their attitudes. These, for her, are attitudes of − at its psychological source the love may be whole and rational, while its compelled or persuaded objectives of childhood become known as the true meaning of her distortions. In short, she treats their attitudes towards ego or interpersonal relations as though they were her own.

The primary problem of personal psychology, in this circumstance, is not transference of distorted love. To take this view of it, on the contrary, tends to set her personal self even deeper into the reflected attitudes of her family, only this time in response to fictive personifications of her psychoanalyst. The problem, rather, involves processes and patterns of transference tightly bound to familial attitudes that move her to distort love as well as other feelings, thoughts and attitudes. The problem is fundamentally to discover why she still holds the relations of ego or interpersonal self she inherited as though they were tested and true in her own contemporaneous present, why she still holds the beliefs, values and ideals first encountered in her childhood environment as though, without reflection, they were valid and reliable in this same present. It is, in sum, to learn why she does not more clearly perceive who really owns the feelings, thoughts and attitudes now, why she does not generally accord her own postfamilial experience at least equal commitment. In this perspective, her distorted love may be seen as a developmental index to the more critical problem of striving for further individuality and self-direction, then forming new relations as ego or interpersonal self, finally integrating them as social self. By using function, it is possible more simply to observe transference directly manifesting familial rather than individual origins of psychological disturbance.

Even when transference of distorted love becomes so embedded in the working inquiry as to appear intractable in resistance, using function together with genesis makes its transformation more effective. In this way, the psychoanalyst may avoid the dead-end of coercive procedure. Note again that both postulates can be applied before explanatory theory or interpretive meta-psychology. Instead of simply making the id interpretation she presumably has to believe in order to resolve her distortions, he may now openly involve her ego or interpersonal self in inquiry into transference turned resistance. And both may respond more directly to their shared experience and extend the focus of their shared inquiry to tacit and manifest evidences of transference and countertransference love. In taking this postulate of function a step further, they may find that transference of love turned resistance reflects the psychoanalyst's own difficulty with familial attitudes in his childhood. Or in uncritical accord with the psychogenetic practice of id therapy (usually signifying a serious commitment of both participants), they may even find that the psychoanalyst tacitly encourages transference of distorted love because it secures the biological model he needs to support his interpretive work with her.

To summarize this point, when genesis prevails in postulate analysis, it turns psychoanalytic inquiry away from actual conditions and ongoing processes and patterns of transference, away from psychic as distinct from social origins of neurosis and, in accordance with the biological model, away from genuine individuality and self-direction. Id metapsychology at the heart of this model, however, is limited with respect to the individual psyche. I again refer to this limitation as it appears in the ego and interpersonal perspectives of the sociological model in Chapter 4 and discuss the notion of individual psyche as it relates to current controversies over the notions of experience and behavior in Chapter 6. I now turn to the other important postulate of id therapy, that of dynamism.

In elaborating the first psychoanalytic model, Freud defended his very strong belief in biological etiology derived from his early study of the hysterias with hypnosis and cathartic therapy. He broke with Breuer, it is well known, over this belief. He sought to gain assent for it with extraordinary single-mindedness, in various contexts terming it psychosexuality, libido theory, dialectic of eros and thanatos, determinism of psychological events or simply id. But reconsider here a rare statement he made in 1915, "The study of the sources of instinct is outside the scope of psychology . . . I am altogether doubtful whether work upon psychological material will afford any decisive indication for the distinction and classification of instincts."* This, and a new but short-lived statement of instinct or drive theory as satisfaction of need, could have been written twenty-five years later by any psychoanalyst working in either the ego or interpersonal wing of the sociological model. Why he did not pursue this fresh approach to the problem of instincts in terms of satisfying needs — very similar, of course, to the interpersonal phrasing — is an interesting

---

*Freud, S.: Instincts and their vicissitudes. In *Collected Papers.* London, Hogarth, 1925, vol. 4, pp. 66-67.

question but, from our present vantage point, still unanswerable.

In order to penetrate the essence of neurosis, the id psycho-analyst consistently invokes the dynamic point of view and transforms psychological events for interpretation as id impulses. In line with this, he even names the problem of his general inquiry neurosis or psychoneurosis, suggesting neurology or physiology as his field of inquiry. But he is, in fact, working within a psychological field of experience, suggesting psychosis as the name of his problem instead. This fuzziness of nomenclature is not his alone. It extends into other psychotherapies that also fail to demarcate these two fields of inquiry from one another. But on grounds never made explicit, he even assumes the translatability of one field of event, structure of inquiry and principle of interpretation into the other. The dynamic point of view, nevertheless, is important for the biological model, bridging a patient's transference of love and her psychoanalyst's id perspective on why she distorts it. The underlying cause of her transference, in this point of view, is her quest for sexual relations on a distorted basis. Her transference, in short, is determined by aim-distorted sexual instincts that are obviously biological. His therapeutic effort, then, is to recover childhood experience of current wishes, reconstruct a genetic history of their distortion, reinterpret them in accordance with id metapsychology and, in the course of this effort, conquer her resistance to it.

Indispensible though it may be for historical purposes, it is clear that genesis falls short of making id interpretations universal. This postulate asks when, where and with whom the sexual wishes first emerged, for these are genetic questions. It does not ask why they do so, for this is the dynamic question. And neither, indeed, asks whether they really do emerge in childhood, for this is beyond question. Obviously, dynamism far outweighs most other postulates in interpretive importance for the biological model. The whole point of instinctual determination is to state in principle what cannot be stated with proof — namely, the empirical and systematic grounding of psychology in biology. This principle, of course, also implies that psychoanalysis is not yet capable of becoming a field of inquiry on its own. No matter what self-sufficiency the study of human psyche may attain in the biological model, it is at some point undercut by this nagging impulse to root psychology in biology. In id therapy, adequate psychological explanation is never enough; interpretation based on biology must also inform the experience.

Regardless of its constructive intent, such interpretation oversimplifies relations among ongoing psychological processes and patterns. But, even temporarily suspending the dynamic point of view, consider transference of love without id metapsychology. It may instead be treated as an overflow of experience distorted to convey dimensions of dependency and anxiety — perhaps panic and at times terror — that she can communicate in no equally telling way to her id psychoanalyst who, of course, best understands them in terms of the id. In this therapeutic inquiry, countertransference provides unconscious support, as well, for the persistent transference of such material. To keep the empirical and systematic issue straight here, it is useful to assume the id psychoanalyst is reasonably sane and well enough integrated. Nothing is ever gained from judging a whole psychoanalytic perspective as the product of personal psychological disturbance — not, at any rate, in substantive terms. Even if that were confirmed beyond doubt, questions about the truth and merit of the perspective itself would still remain.

Consider further that transference of love communicates something a patient cannot otherwise communicate to her id psychoanalyst for whom, especially, biological metaphor has great interpretive power. For what is, after all, more distorted than confessing love and sexual interest to a psychoanalyst deeply engaged in serious psychological inquiry? Interpreting this confession as instinctually determined and then aligning it with id metapsychology may provide for a sense of reality and substance which, if truly biological, no psychological inquiry could ever possibly provide. But the interpreted origin turns out to be, in fact, only speculated metaphor. As a result of making a mysterious jump from the psychological to the metaphorical, the id procedure becomes arbitrary and authoritarian. It becomes arbitrary. No empirical and systematic psychoanalytic inquiry requires a biological interpretation of the psychoanalytic experience overall. It becomes authoritarian. No canon of logic or empiricism in psychoanalytic metapsychology supports the jump from psychology to biology or prevents a further jump to myth and mysticism, cosmology and the occult, utopia and erewhon. Any psychoanalytic metapsychologist is free to select his interpretive categories as he sees them; he may even find some beliefs, values and ideals more congenital than others on grounds far removed from all scientific psychology. But after exercising this freedom to choose metapsychology while pursuing a scientific view of psychoanalysis, he cannot then claim for his jump from psychology to biology, and elsewhere, the logical grounds of empirical and systematic psychoanalysis.

In psychology as distinct from metapsychology, the postulate of dynamism may be paired with that of structure. This postulate may be used for studying id or need satisfaction, ego defense or interpersonal security, or individual psyche and its direction, as these are built into patterns of relatedness that make up the patient's personality. A rounded study requires consideration of structure, in addition to dynamism and the others, for it delineates the ways the patient has grown accustomed to relating on a regular basis. It is, accordingly, often found that it is not that her psyche is distorted in love or fear but rather that she possesses such distorted patterns of transference, resistance and anxiety. This is why structure, in actual inquiry, goes well with dynamism. The pairing of structure and dynamism, like the other two pairings of genesis and function and immediacy and reflection, derives from a general view of human experience as intelligible and orderly. Structure, in this context, answers the question of what pattern is being related to what others in the organization of personality. Dynamism answers the question of why that particular pattern is being enacted. Stated as the dynamic point of view, the why question is not a strictly psychological one in id therapy. Nor, as the first structural point of view, is the what question. Their answers are to be sought outside psychology, essentially in id impulse, instinctual dialectics, drive reduction or energy transformation.

This is the highest level of development of the biological model of psychoanalytic therapy. Freud most fully outlined it in his 1915-1917 *Introductory Lectures* and never substantially changed it. That outline portrays the full sense and adequacy of the biological model of therapy into the early 1930's, as set forth in the *New Introductory Lectures.* Instead of reconstructing therapeutic procedure during the intervening years, he devoted himself to restating many metapsychological issues concerning the dialectics of id impulse, and mainly to developing his new metapsychology of aggression and destruction as the death instinct. But when in the early 1920's, he extended the structural point of view beyond the id to both the ego and the superego, he did not proceed to a conscious extension of the procedures of id therapy as well. This task became the inheritance of his successors, with some continuing to practice the biological model of id impulse and others moving into a new sociological model of ego or interpersonal relation.

It is now possible to see why ego and interpersonal psychoanalysts propose and apply additional postulates for analyzing transference of love. In terms of defense mechanism or security operation, they pursue a functional and structural study beyond the genetic and dynamic study of instincts or needs. But the special power of this second major model, since the 1930's, is to treat processes and patterns that are not id biology and cannot be so construed even by the wildest stretch of imaginative metapsychology. In this, it is also possible to see why they use dynamism apart from exclusive ties to the id. They restate this postulate so that it does not support any one established or evolving metapsychology. Originally emphasized together with genesis in the biological model, it now also applies in such diverse interpretive perspectives as struggle for power, collective unconscious, absolute will, and so on. Seen in this way, every postulate remains a thoroughly psychological tool throughout the therapeutic inquiry.

But interpretive metapsychologies, at present, are not only biological and sociological; they are also psychological — that is, essentially pluralistic, diverse and individual. When the patient, for example, transfers love to her id psychoanalyst, he treats it as a symptom of genetic and dynamic disturbance. The reasons for her doing this, however, may be found in the complex experience of what she resists and is anxious about in her personal psychology.

While continuing to work with such transference, the ego or interpersonal psychoanalyst in the sociological model focuses on this resistance in accordance with structure and function. And while continuing to work with transference and resistance, the psychoanalyst of shared experience, in the psychological model, focuses on this anxiety in accordance with immediacy and reflection. But the id psychoanalyst does not take these later postulate approaches to her resistance or anxiety, resting his therapeutic case with genetic and dynamic analysis of transference in biological terms.

When followers of id metapsychology, using Freud's later statements of id, ego and superego, begin to modify the biological model, the postulate of structure acquires more significance than ever before. For as a result of their pioneering effort, the analysis of resistance — radically distinct, of course, from its conquest — finally comes into its own. First there was Reich's character analysis, then Anna Freud's mechanisms of ego defense, finally Hartmann's ego adaptation; and the ego wing of the sociological model exists by 1940.* Considering similar empirical and systematic material, with different patients and different perspectives on metapsychology, Fromm, Horney, Sullivan and Thompson produce the interpersonal wing of this model by 1940, as well.† The significant aspect dividing them is that the former reach out to sociology and the latter reach in to biology. Ego therapists moving out from biology and interpersonal therapists moving in from sociology cross paths in the analysis of resistance, termed, respectively, ego defense mechanism and interpersonal security operation. In all varieties of ego or interpersonal therapy, despite this difference in metapsychology, while genesis remains no less important than in id therapy, it is now supplemented by a fine-tooth comb study of ego defenses or

---

*For representative works of this wing, see Freud, A.: *The Ego and the Mechanisms of Defense.* New York, International Universities, 1946; Hartmann, H.: *Ego Psychology and the Problem of Adaptation.* New York, International Universities, 1958; Reich, W.: *Character Analysis.* New York, Orgone, 1945.

†And of this wing, see Fromm, E.: *Escape from Freedom.* New York, Rinehart, 1941; Horney, K.: *The Neurotic Personality of Our Time.* New York, Norton, 1937; Sullivan, H.: *Conceptions of Modern Psychiatry.* Washington, W. A. White Psychiatric Foundation, 1947; Thompson, C.: *Psychoanalysis.* New York, Hermitage, 1950.

interpersonal securities — in sum, resistances.

The practice of this new sociological model, of course, gives rise to other sorts of difficulty not recognized until the early 1950's. The ego or interpersonal psychoanalyst, for example, still excludes study of countertransference, counterresistance and counter-anxiety from the field of therapeutic inquiry so that not unlike the id experience, he and his patient do not explore the actual processes and patterns in sequence, only selected outward manifestations. Or as a direct result, he ordinarily turns his patient back on his own experience as though transference, resistance or anxiety took place in a contemporaneous vacuum. In response to such difficulties with the sociological model, psychoanalysis of individual and shared experience is later developed, and I discuss the psychological model in Chapter 8. But it is in the careful, thorough functional and structural analysis of resistance as an adjunct to the genetic and dynamic analysis of transference of id therapy, that ego and interpersonal psychoanalysts make their lasting contribution, and I turn to that next.

Chapter 3

THE SOCIOLOGICAL MODEL

THE sociological model is made up of two wings. In one, psychoanalysts extend the vision and metapsychology of id therapy; in the other, they abandon that vision in favor of cultural, interpersonal metapsychology. They divide into two independent and competitive wings, essentially, according to whether they continue the biological categories already established or, in addition, use openly sociological categories. But they differ mainly about perspective and terminology, rather than observation and definition — a convergence in clinical inquiry the more remarkable for being made from such divergent points of view.

In the ego wing, after Reich's technique of character analysis, Anna Freud's compendium of ego defenses and Hartmann's study of ego adaptation, those reconstructing the biological model take a fresh look at mechanisms of defense and sexual wishes. In the interpersonal wing, after Fromm's crossing of sociology with psychoanalysis, Horney's study of the neurotic personality of our time, Sullivan's study of the interpersonal self system and Thompson's distinction of real from distorted transference in therapeutic inquiry, those constructing the explicitly sociological model also take a fresh look at operations for security and lust dynamisms. In both wings, however, the more they concentrate on analysis of resistance as subject matter of extended inquiry, the less they speculate about any such universal determinism as that claimed for id metapsychology.

It is instructive to place these converging perspectives against the background of the earlier biological model. Consider the following synopsis: in response to transference of love, the id psychoanalyst, in effect, informs his patient that she wants sexual relations with her father, not with him; that since she misperceives him as though he were her father, she now experiences those sexual wishes to be as intolerable yet inescapable as she once did in childhood. Simple and clear, indeed, but it is based on the suggestive procedures of hypnosis and cathartic therapy. In the interest of orderly presentation, I leave further discussion of the psychology of suggestion to Chapter 10.

The id patient here is interpreted into the dilemma of first, no longer being that child whose incestuous wishes were not then satisfied and second, having a psychoanalyst who now satisfies neither the child's nor the adult's wishes because he is a scientist and therapist. But notice the manipulative aspect of this procedure. In order to help her with this two-sided dilemma, he promises that if she recalls early memories of sexual involvement with her father, she will resolve that current fixation of libido on her psychoanalyst and, finally, see him as he really is. But if, in id metapsychology, her transference of love is interpreted as an unconscious manipulative pattern with the distorted aim of having sexual relations with him, may his analysis then be interpreted as an unconscious manipulative pattern with the counterdistorted aim of avoiding them with her?

Regardless of metapsychology, certain questions about transference of love still remain. Does a patient, for example, actually want sexual relations with her id psychoanalyst in the therapeutic present? Or does she persist in expressing sexual wishes to the point of transference resistance because though respecting him, she may also disagree, yet see no other equally telling way to communicate it? To call such questions transference resistance, of course, is a very inventive piece of interpretation supporting psychosexuality. In light of this, the id psychoanalyst's prevailing use of genesis now appears, moreover, to serve him well, if unexpectedly, as counterresistance to his patient's current sexual wishes. By appealing to genesis, he actually redirects his patient's attention to childhood memories of her father and does so in a consistent, self-respecting way. But in this use of genesis as tacit counterresistance, he most likely adds transference power to sexual wishes that, if taken at face value, they might not otherwise acquire in the therapeutic present.

This procedure, of course, is in full accord with the biological model discussed in Chapter 1. In that field of therapy, when the patient becomes engaged in the inquiry, she develops some special quantity of biological impulse seeking discharge. Her libido then flows out toward the psychoanalyst. By the early 1920's, it is no longer a simple therapeutic assumption, however, that she wishes sexual intercourse and this alone. Nor is it so clear by then that such wishes are the major source of her malaise or anxiety, nor that mere satisfaction of them will cure her. The coparticipant experience can no longer be so easily analyzed, because its meanings are no longer so directly intuited. This is so because the new definition of anxiety as function of the ego, among other things, indicates that transference even of sexual wishes is beyond the pleasure principle. Rather than interpret such transference in terms of simple id impulses — which as noted in Chapter 2 are outside the psychological field — it may now be explained in terms of complex ego relations.

From this point onward, no psychoanalytic patient need ever again be treated in the biological model unreconstructed. The id patient may for the first time enter the experiential field of therapy as more fully human. She will openly possess ego or interpersonal self and manifest significant ego functions or interpersonal dynamisms in transference and resistance. Gone is the flesh and blood puppet of id therapy pushed and pulled on a libidinal string, first in childhood by her father in accordance with inevitable psychosexuality, then in therapy by her id psychoanalyst in accordance with inevitable transference love. But with changes in the earlier physiological theory of anxiety, practice of id therapy becomes unwieldy and contradictory in the extreme. For why, if sexual relations are not the patient's objective, does she so distort her relations to her psychoanalyst during therapeutic inquiry now? No id psychoanalyst does nor can know because he continues as late as the 1930's to affirm psychosexuality without change in therapeutic procedure, even after revising the ego and id and redefining anxiety as ego function in the 1920's.

As response to this state of affairs, ego psychologists and interpersonal relationists enlarge the 1915-1917 biological model along distinct yet similar lines. For present purposes, the main difference between ego and interpersonal therapy may be limited to metapsychology and the interpretive consequences that derive from, and at the same time insulate, these two perspectives from one another. In their respective terminologies, both focus new attention on the clinical study of resistance, neither surrenders the biological base of id metapsychology and each adds and extends the new emphasis on social adaptation. Especially with respect to resistance, however, they agree most. They both treat manifestations of resistance as empirically observable and definable — in short, psychoanalyzable — and not as unwelcome obstacles to id interpretation to be conquered and overcome.

In the sociological model, psychoanalysts not only split into two wings of metapsychology but they also begin to work more closely with the outward armor, persona or facade of integrative patterns of personality. To this end, they discontinue the interpretation of transference and resistance solely in terms of id impulse and instinctual drive, need and energy transformation. Instead, they see them as processes and patterns to be observed and defined as essentially egoic and interpersonalized. And they select them from the gross experience of personality formed across a large span of time in countless relations to others. In this new model, the main emphasis is on ego mechanisms and interpersonal dynamisms toward the main objective of reconstructing and readapting ongoing relations between the self and others.

Whatever the residual merits of libido as metapsychology, both ego and interpersonal psychoanalyst agree to disallow it in empirical and systematic inquiry. Some merely set it aside; others vigorously reject it; none make meter readings of its "electric charge."* Nor, as corollary, do they have to determine the appropriate ego or interpersonal patterns for discharging this metapsychological quantity. It is also clear that id and ego psychoanalysts are finally unable to determine whether the earliest ego develops out of the id or apart from it. They therefore become arbitrary about it, no doubt guided by the judgment that one belief helps them to see further psychoanalytically than the other. The issue is, of course, ultimately metapsychology for the interpersonal psychoanalysts as well. But in actual therapeutic inquiry, those who prefer the sociological to the biological model then not only uncover previously neglected aspects of personality

---

*Freud, S.: The defense neuropsychoses. In *Collected Papers* London, Hogarth, 1924, vol. 1, pp. 75.

— especially, resistance and its sequellae — but even discover a new patient.

Psychoanalysis of resistance is the opening wedge for their common breakthrough into new therapeutic ground from different points of view. Once character armor, ego defense or security operation — collectively, resistance — becomes valid for therapeutic inquiry, it is but a short step to the beliefs, values and ideals a patient would defend or secure himself against — secure or defend for himself. This new approach changes the relation of resistance to transference and as a result the overall structure of inquiry. Clinical study of defense or security may, of course, be traced to early 1890's psychoanalytic statements in military metaphor that urge its conquest essentially in order to get rid of it. And in the 1915 to 1917 biological model, the point of this metaphor remains the same — that is, to clear the way for the main agenda of oedipal interpretation of transference. But the psychoanalysis of resistance does not result in actual revisions of procedure until, as developed in the sociological model by 1940, resistance itself defines observations to be made, transformed, explained and interpreted. All this is on a par with transference, the original and focal definition of the biological model.

Since ego and interpersonal therapies share this new empirical concern with resistance, in addition to the new adaptive point of view mentioned earlier, I hyphenate them as ego-interpersonal. In so doing, I do not, of course, equate the two. This follows from the distinction in psychoanalytic structure of explanatory theory, about which both wings agree; and from interpretive meta-psychology, about which they disagree. But I do identify their clinical interests in observation and definition of resistance as well as extending inquiry to transference of the ego or interpersonal self. Although they think about the same clinical material differently (one expanding the biological model into social dimensions, the other expounding cultural and interpersonal terms of the sociological model), they obviously share the new 1930's study of the structure and function of both transference and resistance. Language and terminology aside, similarities are far more critical than differences. Consider first that both retain the biological emphasis — one as id, the other as need — and make it the cornerstone of their respective metapsychologies; second, that both pursue the new study of structure and function in the experiential field of therapy; and third, that both accept the psychoanalytic theory of unconscious or dissociated experience to govern their conduct of therapeutic inquiry.

In this second major model, psychosexuality becomes a particularly troublesome and embarrassing issue, a source of such obfuscations as feminine mystique and masculine myth. While ego-interpersonal perspectives modify and enlarge the biological model, they continue to rely on biological metaphor and supplement it with social and cultural metaphor. But they also reflect differences between European and American attitudes toward personality development. One still seeks significant id impulses in childhood; the other finds significant lust dynamisms in pubescence and identity crises in adolescence. Though metapsychology, id and lust themes still filter through empirical and systematic constructions of therapeutic inquiry, it is troublesome. In practice, both wings confront each other in strategies of statemate, one affirming, the other denying, the biological character of relatedness and communication; so it is also embarrassing. There is, however, no way known to lead out of this ego-interpersonal stalemate; and it remains unknown because the nature of psychological differences between men and women is also still unknown. In the sociological model, such differences are destined to remain unknown because they are not themselves major topics of interest and study. Their sociology and their cultural impact on ego or interpersonal self, in contrast, are far more interesting metapsychology.

Ego-interpersonal psychoanalysis, then, cannot provide a hard scientific basis for differences between men and women. Nor, in fact, does any other strictly psychological inquiry. Although psychoanalysis does not provide for these differences, it does not follow that they are beyond discovery in such other sciences as biology and sociology. It does follow as working hypothesis, rather, that empirical and systematic psychoanalysis simply do not yet encompass their study. This is true in its (1) observation, (2) definition, (3) postulation or (4) theory. Instead of putative differences, these orders of psychoanalytic structure do provide for psychological differences among human beings but only insofar as these appear in the actual terms and conditions of a psychoanalytic inquiry. In view of this, psychoanalysts best treat the unconscious psychology of human beings who happen to be male or female, infant or child, juvenile or pubescent, adolescent or adult. They also go beyond these biological features such as: married to single, rich or poor, democratic or authoritarian, responsible or exploitative, civil rightist or white backlash, cool or square, dove or hawk, theist or atheist and so on.

At present, most psychoanalytic interpretation and speculation about biology and sociology are so generalized as to extend their metaphor, in a serious sense, beyond even the sciences of biology and sociology. Regardless of structure of inquiry, practical considerations often require the psychoanalyst as social being and caring human at work with a patient to adopt certain common-sense attitudes about the very differences that his structure of inquiry does not make known or knowable. In accordance with it, these common-sense attitudes belong at the order of (5) metapsychology. In this way, it is possible to invoke a variety of attitudes toward these differences without, as a rule, obscuring the psychology of processes and patterns studied at the four orders of (1) observation, (2) definition, (3) postulation and (4) theory. The strictly psychological differences between men and women, to date, are beyond the empirical and systematic range of actual psychoanalytic inquiry.

But the ego-interpersonal psychoanalyst still appeals beyond the psychological level, however, to biological and social factors for forces and reinforcers of consensual adaptation. As he expands id therapy into ego-interpersonal areas of interpretation, he eventually adds the role of professional expert to that of father image and introduces patients to beliefs, values and ideals that promise the well-adapted, in addition to the well-adjusted, life. Laudable though his quest for efficient and effective therapy may be, it clearly overshadows the range of actual psychological inquiry demarcated by the four orders mentioned above and discussed in greater detail in Chapter 7. Primarily interested in making personality change, as distinct from exploring the psychological processes and patterns of its change, the therapist lapses into a chronic case of therapeutic furor for which the best prophylaxis, now, is desire to know the ways of human psyche with direct attitudes of curiosity about them. In other words, his pragmatics of therapy are always so much more important than anything else that they threaten to displace the syntactics of his inquiry. And this, of course, points up a major source of manipulation in the sociological model.

In the new study of resistance, metapsychology loses the singular and uniform character it once had in the biological model. The split into two major wings, of course, helped to bring this about, and it is a significant advance. But some psychoanalysts, practicing id therapy unreconstructed, continue to conquer and overcome resistances. Others, without leaving the biological perspective, so modify it as to secure autonomous functions of the ego and its defense mechanisms. Still others, treating similar clinical material as security operations, attempt to interpersonalize metapsychology altogether along the lines of sociology and anthropology. To appreciate this growing variability of metapsychology, consider the following political analogy: conservatives seek to retain the biological model in its original form; liberals retain its id perspective but also accommodate the new empirical study of ego in resistance; progressives respond to social and economic upheavals of the 1930's and undertake therapy with previously untouchable schizoid and schizophrenic personalities.

To round out the picture and suggest the radical thrust of the contemporary psychological model considered in Chapter 8, it is instructive to extend the analogy. Now that psychoanalysis has strong enough empirical and systematic foundations, the biological and sociological perspectives no longer distinguish its therapeutic inquiry. It is mature enough, so to speak, to molt the two wings of ego and interpersonal metapsychology in favor of a solid footing in pluralism and diversity and focus more directly on the psychology of unconscious experience, its field of inquiry. As a result of this increased solidity, its structure of inquiry may, moreover, do without the anterior support of any single established metapsychology. In addition to satisfying id needs and maintaining ego-interpersonal securities, it is possible to see the terms, conditions and outcomes of psychoanalytic inquiry itself as the critical concern of the psychological model. For once id needs are biologically adjusted and ego-interpersonal securities socially adapted, psychological questions still remain. What about the well-adjusted and the well-adapted who do the consensually expected and still suffer anxieties, depressions and other miseries? Or what about that largely uncharted, inner stretch of their psyches? But this is getting ahead of the story.

The ego-interpersonal patient does not live out the push-and-pull effects of id impulse in a direct correspondence of one to one; on the other hand, he is not the more fully human person he may yet become in the psychological model. He is, in all, a new patient who presents new therapeutic concerns about reconstructing ego mechanisms or interpersonal dynamisms and about redirecting id or need satisfactions in accordance with the average, expectable or consensually validated environment. Nor, of course, does his psychoanalyst interpret their meanings as solely determined by glandular function and discharge; he views their formation and forward movement in the perspective of social conditioning, instead. And he prefers developing a detailed ego-interpersonal biography to relying on extravagant biological metaphor which is also a major step toward mature psychoanalysis. But he does not make it all the way. In addition to the id or needs satisfied in the biological model he now treats his patients as a constellation of social securities defended (as, in short, a kind of ego-interperson) but lacking a category of individual psyche and its direction, does not see him emerging in personal fulfillment.

Denial of individuality or uniqueness to the human psyche sharply focuses the manipulative and synthetic aspects of the sociological model. As one significant clinical result, any ego-interpersonal patient's direct response is not considered worthy of direct response in turn. What is wrong with him, generally, then, is far more welcome therapeutic inquiry than what is right with him. Following the id tradition, the ego-interpersonal psychoanalyst sees himself as primarily reactive, rarely active, in relation to his patient. He ordinarily sees himself as reactive through the armor, persona or facade of his professional expertise and, of course, cautions against looking at countertransference in the immediate contexts in which it becomes manifest. As a professional expert, he not only does not participate in study of a patient's perceptions of his psychoanalyst's distortions but he actively discourages this study in the therapeutic field of their occurrence. This view, to say the least, is incompatible with the new empirical advances of the sociological model. Even in avowedly ego-interpersonal study, the psychoanalyst finds it appropriate to turn a facade of expert indifference to certain observations his patient makes of their shared experience. This reluctance to look at countertransference when and as it emerges during inquiry, no matter what the metapsychologies, remains an unwritten chapter in the history of psychoanalysis; it will not soon yield to clear statement of its psychological origins.

In the sociological model, a patient learns to view his experience as ego-interpersonal apparently without expecting a psychoanalyst to view his the same way. That is, he cannot expect any exploratory response from his coparticipant about the experience of countertransference. All he can do about this, obviously, is take it for what it is worth and move on to greener psychological pastures. But there is still something distant, detached and half-hearted about the participant observer of ego-interpersonal relations who, on principle, never turns observed participant during the experience and arbitrarily disengages when his patient observes him participating. These comments, of course, do not refer to a particular psychoanalyst responding for a particular reason to a particular patient but rather to the standard procedure of ego-interpersonal therapy. Proposed as a tentative hypothesis, to be considered in the next chapter, this therapy does not directly explore countertransference with the patient as participant observer because it is not primarily a psychological inquiry. In trying to bring about social and ego-interpersonal change of personality above all else, it removes their ego-interpersonal relations from the firsthand actualities of psychoanalytic experience.

On its face, avoidance of countertransference is grossly incongruous with this pyschoanalyst's general aim of demythologizing intensive psychotherapy. To see why he does not make observation of himself participating adjunct to his participation observing a patient, recall the clinical example used to illustrate the biological model. Take the case of the patient, again, whose sexual wishes obviously cannot be satisfied within any psychological approach to psychoanalytic therapy. If the ego-interpersonal psychoanalyst, extending the biological model, no longer conceives her sexual wishes as the motive force of transference, it is no longer clear that he also has to hold the id line against considering countertransferred attitudes towards these wishes as part of the therapeutic inquiry in which they emerge.

If, in other words, transference of character traits, ego mechanisms or interpersonal dynamisms are now appropriate for inquiry, why forbid the study of countertransference of these very same processes and patterns in each case? Why are certain processes and patterns somehow still privileged in the psychoanalytic experience simply because of the coparticipant who happens to possess them? In the sociological model, however, even with respect to countertransference of love, so long as the ego-interpersonal psychoanalyst can remain genuine and objective and seriously committed to its study, what possible psychological grounds suffice to exclude it? When countertransference interferes with the therapeutic effort in specific contexts of inquiry, and if a particular patient is capable of observing its relation to emerging themes of inquiry, why forbid this exploration as well? Either active or passive denial here can have only negative effects on a patient's future openness to psychoanalysis of resistance — presumably the new and major concern of ego-interpersonal therapy.

Regardless of a particular psychoanalyst's answers, these questions point up an unworkable contradiction peculiar to the sociological model itself. On the one hand, innovators in both wings expand therapeutic inquiry to include ego functions or interpersonal dynamisms capable of aligning id or need satisfactions with the overall direction of personality. At the same time, they honor the older tradition of excluding countertransference, even though that tradition serves a biological model not yet capable of studying id impulse in relation to ego function. The sociological model, in this respect, is a case of new theory inadequately realized in practice. Failing to confront this but instead conferring fictive facades on psychoanalyst and patient (one provides, the other receives services; one psychoanalyzes, the other is psychoanalyzed) the sociological model sets manipulative elements into its procedure. It fails to observe and openly work with countertransference within the experiential field of its emergence.

The ego-interpersonal psychoanalyst, however, need not have faced the absolute choice between avoiding countertransference and terminating therapy. He, of course, no longer saw counter-transference arising from biology of id impulse apart from sociology of ego-interpersonal relation. But if he had consistently worked out the new formulations of ego defense and interpersonal security, he might also have applied them to counterresistance, no less than resistance. Firmly in the experiential field of therapy, it is the ego-interpersonal self, psychoanalyst's or patient's, that expands psychoanalysis of transference, that creates psycho-analysis of resistance and that could have created psychoanalysis of countertransference and counterresistance in relation to them. So if as a function of ego-interpersonal self, resistance need no longer be simply conquered and overcome, neither does counter-resistance; and if transference no longer simply masks and disguises sexual wishes, neither does countertransference. From this it follows that keeping countertransference from the experiential field of therapy, first in the biological model, then in the sociological model, is not consistent with the new observations and perspectives. By identifying his own role as professional expert, the ego-interpersonal psychoanalyst, in effect, obeys his id predecessor's injunction against acknowledging it, let alone studying it.

Neither expertise based on trained experience nor authority based on traditional procedure is relevant to this critical issue. It is, rather, that the expert interposes his authority between transference and countertransference in support of the con-ventional double standard for therapist and patient in the same experience. Beyond conventional wisdom, however, is still that field of psychic experience they share with each other and the rest of humanity — if in truth, not mere epigram, we are all trying to become more simply human than otherwise. Does a psychoanalyst's experience suffice, then, for his authority to take over the inquiry? Or does he instead rely on irrational symbols of status and power with a disturbed individual seeking insight into irrationalities he already bears heavily enough without being confronted with still another set? But in addition to this simple unity of human experience, consider the fundamental question for all models of psychoanalysis. Does the psyche exhibit any hard uniformities of process and pattern that make up a scientific field of inquiry? Or does it dissolve and somehow disappear in the biological, social and ego-interpersonal identity of its possessor?

The ego-interpersonal mode of participant observation is one significant reason for proceeding since then to the psychological model. This mode of observation is psychologically artificial and therefore has awkward effects on ongoing psychoanalytic inquiry. For what expert in ego adaptation or interpersonal security, or even behavior adjustment, can show just where in psychoanalysis of human psyche or science of psychology he would draw a clear line in basic psychology between his patient and himself? Nothing in psychoanalytic psychology provides a clear basis for drawing this line; nor does anything in general psychotherapeutic inquiry, for it is mythical and finally irrelevant to the psychoanalytic quest for individuality and self-direction.

But a psychic line between the psychoanalytic coparticipants is also arbitrarily drawn in the biological model, as well. It is, moreover, probable that it has to be so drawn. As long as id impulse is the focus of id therapy, direct psychological relations between psychoanalyst and patient can lead to id relations that, in effect, would terminate the whole inquiry. This is not as farfetched as it may sound, since satisfaction of id impulse is the main interpretive category of the biological model. Such a line is also arbitrarily drawn in the sociological model, and in a similar way. As long as the ego-interpersonal self is the focus of therapeutic inquiry, direct psychological relations between psychoanalyst and patient could lead to ego-interpersonal satisfactions and securities, as well. The terminology of this model is hardly as graphic and romantic as that of its id predecessor. It is dry and impersonal enough to suggest that no ego-interpersonal psychoanalyst involves his patient beyond the requirements of therapeutic inquiry. But it also promises more relatedness than it seems to deliver, for the psychoanalyst's self-assigned role of expert or partner implies a certain scientific detachment in practice, excluding even the ego-interpersonal from his observable role with a patient. His role in ego-interpersonal therapy is, overall, social and not personal; his perspective extends outside and around the category of individual psyche, as though it made no difference whether a human psyche exists at all.

If this arbitrary line between psychoanalyst and patient were also drawn in the contemporary psychological model, it would be done as a hangover from the past. A transference, so to speak, from biological and sociological models into the psychoanalytic present, it could be judged a distortion that covers up the human psyche. Keeping all countertransference, counterresistance and counteranxiety out of the experiential field of therapy (if that, in any significant sense, were possible) would prevent the psychoanalyst from exploring with his patient a two-way experience that they both individuate and participate. Perspectives on metapsychology are now pluralistic and diversified for this same reason. Neither participation nor individuality can, of course, be realized in psychoanalytic inquiry so tied to any one interpretive perspective as to foreclose appeal to all others.

It is, nevertheless, still difficult to undertand tendencies toward manipulation in the sociological model, especially in its own conceptual terms. Even without comparing it to others, this difficulty is clear enough from an internal point of view. Recall again how it enlarges and refines the statement of defense mechanisms and security operations, for the first time breaking psychoanalytic procedure out of one-way regressive concern with childhood trauma and into patterns of personality currently transacting. In this way, it also expands definition of resistance beyond infantile events and fantasies as simply blockades to be overcome. Resistances may be no less numerous and multidimensional and, above all, psychoanalyzable than transferences are already known to be. Not only the id, now, but the ego is also in resistance. So the range of inquiry expands far beyond transference and transference resistance of abbreviated and distorted impulses.

After redefining anxiety as ego-interpersonal function, neither wing of the sociological model fully realizes the possibilities of psychoanalysis of anxiety, as well. Anxiety is still not related to transference or resistance in the sociological model, any more than it is related to transference in the earlier biological model. Anxiety attains its full sense and adequacy as definition on a par with both transference and resistance only in the psychological model, and this new inquiry into anxiety requires two new postulates of immediacy and reflection. For if anxiety is not a psychic representative of physiological excitation to be relieved through direct physical discharge, then its study becomes psychological through and through, and its analysis has special significance for the therapeutic experience. Equally important, the study of counteranxicty also relates to both countertransference and counterresistance, in this way even further expanding the empirical range of psychoanalysis.

Placing these clinical difficulties of the sociological model against the background of its metapsychology, it is helpful to recall that a sense of personal uniqueness or individuality is not among its critical categories. As a result, the patient's concerns about ego-interpersonal adaptation versus psychic individuality are ordinarily pushed to the fringes of therapeutic inquiry. They are perhaps joined there by similar concerns of his psychoanalyst who, even if he resolves them, cannot let on, partly because he does not practice the open study of countertransference and partly because he holds an adaptive, social and cultural perspective on his life experience.

Without this category of individuality or personal uniqueness, the ego-interpersonal psychoanalyst cannot, moreover, conceive a way out of the dilemmas of termination. During the 1930's the topic of terminable and interminable psychoanalysis was thoroughly reconsidered. In view of the new empirical study of resistance, it is clear that if any one psychological process or pattern can serve as defense against any other, then psychoanalysis cannot set psychological guidelines to its terminal point as therapeutic inquiry. Lacking the category of individuality in particular or human psyche in general, both id and ego-interpersonal models of therapy have to posit a basis for that terminal point outside psychology — in, respectively, adjustive biology of id impulse and adaptive sociology of ego-interpersonal relation.

Individual psyche is not only a datum but a factum as well. It is not simply given in terms of being inborn, it is made and matured as a lifelong concern. In shared inquiry that avoids tendencies toward manipulation, no psychoanalyst can act as though its pursuit were relevant to his patient and not to himself — without, in fact counterresisting and also getting into other therapeutic difficulties. No psychoanalyst is immune to pressures of ego-interpersonal identity converging with those of psychic individuality or the other way around. Such pressures may at times also become dominant and so pervade his life experience as, in some form, to recur during therapeutic inquiry when a patient brings his own actual or imagined difficulties about them into question.

Psychoanalysts do not all fit a single pattern of procedure — some engage, others detach; some criticize, others nurture; some study experience, others behavior. It is pointless to seek, here, to establish a common procedure for all. The point is to delineate differences between biology of id impulse and sociology of ego-interpersonal relation and, in turn, between them and the psychology of shared experience. The point now is to see how the category of individuality supplements those of satisfaction and security and extends the structure of psychoanalysis. With this third additional category to guide him, the psychoanalyst may face the hazards and opportunities of open experience with another person, even with a distorted and suffering patient in therapeutic inquiry.

If the ego-interpersonal psychoanalyst had considered relating transference and resistance to counterresistance and counter-transference a live alternative, he would have reconstructed the sociological model of his practice of therapy. And if he had revised its perspective on validation within the average, consensually expected environment, he would have faced the radical diversity of all individuals who actually go through a psychoanalytic inquiry. He might, moreover, have escaped the trap of thinking he could solve the problem of psychological differences between men and women any better than his id predecessor by simply transferring its interpretation from the domain of biology to that of sociology. Instead, he might have treated the problem as psychoanalytic metapsychology — no matter what other scientific or personal interest it nevertheless still retained for him — and accepted the plain empirical limitations of his field of inquiry to resolve it further. I discuss these and other difficulties of ego-interpersonal therapy in the next chapter.

Chapter 4

QUESTIONS ABOUT
EGO-INTERPERSONAL THERAPY

As a result of biologizing metapsychology, psychoanalytic answers to the question of what a woman really wants have so far failed to gain assent. In that well-established model, her psychology is interpreted according to male biology. She must fundamentally overcome penis envy. The ego-interpersonal criticism is essentially to go beyond it to the view that she actually does not want a penis but, because of social and cultural pressures, the power and freedom it symbolizes instead. Starting from a perspective on feminine psychology subordinated to male biology, as id psychoanalysts always discover to their bewilderment, there can be no knowledge of a woman's psychology in her own terms. But the difference between id and ego-interpersonal psychoanalysis revolves, here, about the symbolic merits of evolutionary biology. Beyond this, a primarily human and scientific psychoanalytic psychology may, however, be conceived to follow the lead of its subject matter as found and developed in the experiential field of therapy. For once the biological line of one-dimensional interpretation changes, the argument from social and cultural pressures falls flat. It is, then, not hard to clear up the mystery of this nineteenth-century Freud-Darwin woman who suffers from penis envy.

In a perspective that does not base its interpretive power on evolutionary or social biology, something new begins to happen. On a psychological level, a woman's wants, interestingly enough, do not much differ from a man's. It soon becomes clear that she wants what any human being wants and, in any case aside from sexual differences, that some human wants can never be satisfied under conditions of psychoanalytic therapy. In larger perspective, what she wants is not the only or most telling question about her psychology. Her beliefs and hopes, values and fantasies, ideals and despairs and the relations of her psyche to her biology, sociology and ego-interpersonality are no less telling questions. During psychoanalytic inquiry, they are, of course, just as applicable to a man's psychology. Being human, she seeks a system of beliefs, values and ideals; and being psychoanalyzed, she seeks as clear and thorough a reading of her conscious and unconscious experience as this structure of inquiry can make. In the psychological model, the question of what does a particular patient, woman or man, really wants can only be answered in the therapeutic field in which it arises, when and as it actually does.

In Chapter 2, I discussed some aspects of the problem of transference of love in id therapy. However, equally difficult is the ego-interpersonal position, again mainly as a matter of meta-psychology. If consensual adaptation for purposes of defense and security actually does focus the aims of ego-interpersonal experience, then using the sociological model, in a culture that exploits any special group (women, for example), the clear study of that group is not possible from this psychoanalytic point of view. Not that some women practicing ego-interpersonal psychoanalysis, as well as some men, cannot succeed at the psychotherapy of women. But the serious question is whether and, if so, to what extent, it is possible to psychoanalyze women or any other mistreated, exploited and underprivileged social group with a view toward their adaptation. Exponents of biological and sociological models themselves may be most liberal-minded psychoanalysts; yet elements of their models of therapy deriving from biosocial Darwinism fail, rather, to project a vision of human experience beyond the categories of adjustment of id impulse and adaptation of ego-interpersonal relation to their environments. Darwinism, it is clear, has strongly influenced this development in psychoanalysis; but I consider this theme separately in Chapter 5.

In essential outline, the woman's problem with ego-interpersonal therapy may now be stated. She cannot admit contradictory desires for both free individuality and ordered dependency with a professional expert who envelops himself and his views in the irrational symbols of power and authority of their environing culture. If she feels kindly toward him and, moreover, would like to avoid interlockings of anxiety and counteranxiety, she ordinarily does not even touch this painful contradiction in open experience but instead becomes irritable, skittish, edgy, out of sorts and even impossible to understand at that point in the inquiry. She seems to endure conflicted transference to her psychoanalyst's unawareness and in this way, at least maintains the status quo, which the therapist does not ordinarily explore as long as she makes the average id adjustment and expectable ego-interpersonal adaptation. If she does what in agreed consensus she is supposed to do, he judges her transference and resistance reasonably well psychoanalyzed and prepares for termination. For she can now do what she has to do for the necessities of her environment and at times even appear to like it.

Probing this further, it is soon discovered that, as mentioned above, she has difficulty in attaining the incompatible ends of exercising freedom and securing dependency. This difficulty, besides being hers, in some sense pervades all human experience. When in transference or resistance to her psychoanalyst she becomes aware that she truly owns her psyche and no one but herself can really do anything about certain of its inner dimensions, this may emerge as a strange and terrifying awareness. Only on the basis of modifying her dependency can she secure the free conditions for living it out, even with him. For in creating the psychological conditions for living it, she also assumes responsibility for actually having it. But this is not the only source of her anxieties.

Another important source is her awareness that in our culture, assertion is not an especially noteworthy act of love but, rather, aggression. In ego-interpersonal perspectives, assertion may, of course, be so defined as to distinguish it from aggression. It is then difficult to sustain this distinction in actual experience where the two, however imperceptibly, tend to merge into one another. The general ego-interpersonal environment for which this distinction is made to be valid is not, moreover, actually hospitable to it, often overlooking nice differences between the two and looking to hard results alone. On this point, consider Sullivan's view that "we seem to be born . . . with something of this power motive within us."*

---

*Sullivan, H.: *Conceptions of Modern Psychiatry*. Washington, W. A. White Psychiatric Foundation, 1947, p. 6.

The puzzling thing about "this power motive" is whether in his metapsychology, it belongs among biological pursuits of satisfaction or cultural pursuits of security, or somewhere else unknown. As long as it is practically impossible to distinguish the biology from the sociology of "this power motive," it remains practically impossible to distinguish its inner experience as aggression from its outer appearance as assertion. During ego-interpersonal change, such questions, however, do not usually become serious psychoanalytic inquiry.

Such is this patient's situation in the sociological model. In order not to be torn apart as the incompatibilities of freedom and dependency emerge, she tends to distort her relations to her psychoanalyst. Working through them on her own, however, involves her in a deeper experience of her individual psyche, which neither this metapsychology in particular nor this culture at large value very highly or even on a par with satisfaction of id need and defense of ego-interpersonal security. No expert in adaptation can, as a general rule, genuinely understand this patient. The important aspect of struggle which the patient has to let go of, in fact, is tightly embedded in metapsychology which the psychoanalyst has to hold onto. This aspect comprises irrational symbols of social status and prestige that run at least indifferent, but usually counter, to genuine individuality. The ego-interpersonal psychoanalyst can, of course, help this patient. He can and often does within the two categories of satisfying biological needs and maintaining ego-interpersonal securities. To this extent, then, her tendencies toward distortion may be worked through and modified, if not altogether obviated. Within these categories is found the ego-interpersonal existence that both psychoanalyst and patient, at present, consensually accept as the average and expectable development of personality.

In this perspective, the psychoanalyst may actually come to believe that he — his social and ego-interpersonal self, that is — can be the full bearer of his identity. There is a certain grey humor to considering his identity a function of his social security, but a number, literally, without which he cannot be identified as being either social or secure. Since biological and sociological models are foreclosed to the deeply personal miseries about a free psyche and its self-direction (the third category proposed for the psychological model), neither id nor ego-interpersonal psychoanalyst may even be aware that his patient's freedom and dependency, inevitably moving in opposite directions, are probably tearing her sense of individuality apart. Adhering to established perspectives, his best therapeutic tack as professional expert may be silence. Although he obviously cannot work with what he does not perceive or acknowledge, if he leaves her to her own affective and cognitive resources, she may still be able to do it alone. But in his own terms, he cannot get at psychological troubles extending beyond either the biological or the social and ego-interpersonal.

Above, I observed that a woman may not want anything essentially different from what a man wants. Implicit in this observation, of course, is still another fact, namely, that both possess human psyche and strive to fulfill their affective and cognitive endowment. Now I may accordingly add that psychoanalytic struggles over freedom and dependency are just as easily illustrated in terms of either sex. Consider as basic to this view that an empirical and systematic psychology of these differences does not yet exist; above all, that the nature of affective and cognitive differences between men and women is therefore still unknown; and finally, that while the question lingers on, it may ultimately prove to be unanswerable in psychological terms. At present, its fate as science of human psychology is no more interesting than, for example, the 1930's Nazi theory that rationalizes genocide of so-called inferior peoples or the 1960's racist theory that rationalizes white exploitation of colored peoples everywhere. No psychoanalyst, however, can provide the answers here, not because he lacks general and common-sense information but rather because his specific structure of inquiry does not furnish critical and decisive information. In Chapter 8, I consider this limitation of psychoanalysis in regard to beliefs, values and ideals a major reason for constructing the psychological model.

This model, as so far developed, shifts the emphasis from didactic metapsychology to exploratory psychology and, along these lines, from biosocial and ego-interpersonal to psychological perspectives. These two shifts, in turn, support study of human psyche unfolding in the experiential field of therapy, when and as it unfolds, and also check the abuses of preestablished metapsychology. It becomes increasingly clear, as a result, that empirical and systematic psychoanalysis cannot isolate problems of women from problems of men and then reliably treat the one set apart from the other. It also follows that, fundamentally, these problems are neither biosocial nor ego-interpersonal but psychological. Getting down to where psychic resources move and how they emerge, it is not so much what goes on between psychoanalyst and patient as what, in this manner of speaking, comes off them. Moreover, it is the ability to feel and think one's way into the affective and cognitive individuality of his own or the other's psyche, then be able to accept his findings and set them before the experience of the other. This sense of individual psyche and ability to make its resources felt and thought in participant experience tells the difference, finally, between sanity and madness.

Any biosocial or ego-interpersonal disturbance, from this point of view, may be seen as a surface symptom of failed psychology of self-direction, individuality and participation. Whether it takes the diagnosed form of hysteria, obsession, psychosis or schizophrenia, in this view, depends on accidents of birth and anomolies of biography. For the question is always, first and last, whose psyche is at the center of one's life experience. As metapsychology of disturbance, the ego-interpersonal perspective favors, and essentially seeks, clarity of consensual validation in the expectable environment. The psychological model, in this respect as well, goes beyond biosocial and ego-interpersonal issues of distortion, disturbance and difficulty and instead seeks knowledge of the two particular psyches involved in the particular psychoanalytic experience. After exhausting psychological dimensions of inquiry, the patient may take this knowledge into future life and integrate it with his evolving beliefs, values and ideals.

The root difficulty is a curious failure to recognize and respect inherently psychological limits of the structure of psychoanalysis itself. For personal and professional reasons, psychoanalysts tend to take this structure from the field of experience for which it was developed and use it to study problems of biology and society, politics and morals, education and religion it was never intended for. All it can do, in fact, is guide psychological inquiry in depth beyond the biosocial and cultural, and beyond problems, even, of men and women as such, into affective and cognitive resources of human psyche. When conceived as inquiry into fields of relatedness and communication, if psychoanalysis surrenders its essential aim of psychological inquiry, it cannot make a sane claim to being itself. The point of coordinating a structure of psychoanalytic inquiry is to explore unconscious processes and patterns of human psyche; the point of making its order of metapsychology pluralistic, diverse and individual is to assure the widest range of its interpretive application.

Even from so brief a reference to structure of inquiry, it may now be clear that id metapsychology is not set aside because it is wrong; nor is ego-interpersonal metapsychology because it is external. They are instead superseded for the reason that they do not relate therapeutic inquiry directly to psychic resources of individuality and participation and, therefore, personal fulfillment. Though still used as metapsychologies, they even derive from different modes of thought (id impulse from metabiology, ego-interpersonal relation from metasociology) that are heavily weighted with elements of biological and social Darwinism. In any case, these nineteenth-century metaphors do not retain the intellectual force and power they once had; they are being displaced with twentieth-century metaphors of outer-space technology and inner-space psychology. Perhaps since psychoanalysts no longer have to fit their psychological inquiry to preestablished metapsychologies and are less prone to making large judgments beyond their empirical and systematic competence, it may simply be that id and ego-interpersonal metapsychologies have outlived their time and usefulness.

With these issues so much in flux, pluralism in metapsychology makes it possible to interpret psychological problems and resolutions in accordance with a general perspective, yet without having to do so on a priori grounds. Let the patient decide this — freedom to make his own way in the psychoanalytic experience depends on both his and his psychoanalyst's fundamental beliefs, values and ideals — which is not psychology but, of course, metapsychology. It is not possible to so simplify the issues, however, as to make them fit any one metapsychology now established or evolving. It may again become necessary to attempt this at some future date, but that future is not immediate or even proximate. Present diversity of perspectives instead suggests that the psychoanalytic patient does not find it feasible to fit all his experience into his psychoanalyst's symbols and metaphors.

Since metapsychology is, in fact, not decisive or critical for expansion of psychological awareness, perhaps both participants may be fussing about the superiority of one or another perspective because of insecurities and defenses against them. Or after expanding his awareness, a patient may be as pleased to terminate without engaging his psychoanalyst in speculative interpretation. He may even be pleased enough with his psychoanalytic outcome simply to accept certain unalterable differences in metapsychology, just as after studying transference and countertransference, he may also accept certain unalterable differences in psychology and move on from that field of experience. At a deeper level, a patient may understand but at times remain silent about such differences because he finds further inquiry engages his psychoanalyst in repeating still another round of transference and countertransference, resistance and counterresistance, anxiety and counteranxiety, and so on. In an appreciative mood, he may therefore simply let them go with a special personal sense and regard for his psychoanalyst's unique individuality.

Since the first id metapsychology of men and women based on instinct theories, several psychoanalysts have founded several others. These range from struggle for power, collective unconscious and absolute will, to social adaptation, self-realization and ego-interpersonal security to mystical self-love, existentialist anxiety and mysterious self-transcendence. It follows from such diversity that during actual inquiry, it is best to take a pluralistic view of metapsychology such that psychoanalyst and patient need not lock horns over issues still unknown and unknowable. They remain free, nonetheless, to choose and articulate their own views, each in his own individual way. But notice, however, that no matter which one a particular psychoanalyst happens to live and believe, whether listed or, indeed, not yet stated, his empirical and systematic inquiry with any particular patient derives from the same psychoanalytic structure that guides this same inquiry of other psychoanalysts with other patients. It is not a preference in metapsychology that makes his therapy psychoanalytic, it may now be clear, but his overall structure of inquiry. For he may use any one metapsychology in still other psychotherapies, short-term, hypnotic, nondirective, supportive and behavioral, or he can believe it and do nothing at all, in practice, with any psychotherapy.

Generally speaking, psychoanalysts treating men and women often have some difficulty treating the theme of sexuality. In part by culture, in part by metapsychology, in part by patients, they are continually pushed into the awkward position of interpreting psychological differences between men and women without, in fact, having the reliable scientific knowledge to do so. This is not a matter of some psychoanalysts having it, some not, on the basis of superior talent and training, original intuition and experience. It is, rather, an inevitable limitation built into the structure of psychoanalysis itself. The point is that psychoanalytic procedure does not yield the knowledge needed to make these interpretations scientific and reliable. Hence there is the association of feminine mystique and masculine myth with psychoanalytic therapy.

Psychoanalysts at work in the field of relating unconscious to conscious experience may best interpret these psychological relations. But can they, under psychoanalytic conditions, also do scientific study of male and female sexuality? Even when they claim it, the evidence suggests something quite different, namely, that they study some relations of unconscious to conscious psychology within a structured inquiry for which sexuality is neither substantive nor empirical-systematic but at best symptomatic and interpretive-metapsychological. While sexuality may therefore be considered in some sense relevant to the psychoanalytic enterprise, it is only indirectly so. For it has no special relevance to structured inquiry by psychological as distinct from, for example, physiological procedures; nor does psychoanalytic procedure in particular reveal anything special about it, either. As long as psychoanalysis remains essentially a psychological inquiry, its practice cannot be expected to do more. And so long as it does not require belief in any single perspective, Freudian, Adlerian, Jungian, Rankian and so on, then problems of men and women in bed are no more significant, as such, than in the living room, the park, the assembly line, the executive suite, on the road, and so on and on, even in the psychological laboratory and, actually, the experiential field of any psychotherapy.

As already noted, the theme of sexuality reflects lingering influences of nineteenth-century perspectives. They are biological and adaptive, going back to Lamarck, Darwin and Huxley; historical and genetic, going back to Hegel, Marx and Spencer. In their time, they were powerful principles of interpretation. But some questions may be raised about them that require new answers today. Do biological and instinctual theories of Darwin and Freud, for example, continue to provide the same penetrating depth of insight and interpretation? If so, why are established metapsychologies in stalemate within id and ego-interpersonal psychoanalysis? Why are many psychoanalysts and patients now looking elsewhere for more appropriate perspectives and metaphors?

Moreover, do patients still seek psychoanalysis in the suggestible grip of blind hysterics, under the compulsive pressure of deaf obsessions? Or are they becoming ever more alert to deceptions of feminine mystique and distortions of masculine myth, unusually forthright about hypocrisies and falsehoods of the culture, quite aware of seeking individuality, truth and freedom in psychoanalytic experience? And if they cannot escape the insecurities of this radically new era of atomic energy, technology, electronics, expanding human rights and rising cultural aspirations, how can their id and ego-interpersonal psychoanalysts hope to, no matter how closely they stick to metapsychologies of id satisfaction and ego-interpersonal security? Is it possible, now, to interpret one set of psychological conditions with a perspective formulated specifically to cope with another long past?

Instinctual and biological metaphors of the Freud-Darwin vision of human experience do not, it is clear, adequately interpret psychological problems. Not that these metaphors are suddenly proved wrong but rather that they are no longer significantly right; they, in fact, fall short of distinctly human psyche and its experience, individuality and its direction and fulfillment. For metapsychology to be effective, it has to interpret psychological exploration of inner space with a unique set of highly individuated metaphors. But it does not require acceptance of nineteenth-century metapsychology as credential for its validity. It is no longer owned and subsidized by a Victorian middle class that hypocritically condemns public exposure of a lady's ankle yet sees nothing wrong with widespread sexual abuse and perversion being practiced under the cover of social proprieties. Potentially involving the community at large, psychoanalytic psychology is at present rapidly becoming a public enterprise.

What does this indicate about the extravagant interpretive use of sexual and biological metaphors in the past? Essentially, that psychoanalysis once invoked the Freud-Darwin ideologies to show how nineteenth-century idealism and morality could be faked and commercialized and, by interpretation, expose the extent of self-deceptive exploitation in sexual and other human relations. And significantly, that interpretations of sexual life cannot be generalized and applied so far away from the experience being lived and reported in therapy. It is now necessary to treat sexual relations as being, instead, radically individual within each patient's affective and cognitive awareness of how he has, can and will integrate them from a psychological point of view. Sexual relations, in any event, never directly reproduce the individuality and participation that Freud-Darwin metapsychologies assert a patient's biological instincts and cultural environment have made him heir to; not so long, that is, as he appreciates a genuine sense of his individual psyche.

In psychoanalytic perspectives, individuality and participation complement one another. The dialectics of actual inquiry make individuality a function of participation and participation a function of individuality. But this is not all. These terms, and the processes and patterns they represent, also have to be treated substantively. Though one cannot develop without the other, individuality is no less earned, made and created than participation is inborn, given and direct; and the same holds true the other way around. While one emerges in relation to the other, whatever else contributes to its emergence, neither can be said to emerge outside a field of experience. They do not, therefore, have their interpretive meaning packaged and labeled on their surface. The relations of individuality and participation are not fixed by id biology or ego-interpersonal sociology. Basic to all meta-psychology, their great diversities are open to great varieties of expression and meaning. In view of this, notice again that psychoanalytic structure is open at the fifth order to make room for them. More important than this, in response to the current value revolution whose objectives are primarily psychological, psychoanalysis needs to be made available in new and still unreconstructed visions of human experience, which no doubt are now in the making. For once constructed and deeply rooted in the unconscious patterning of cultural experience, these visions may be expected to become as relevant to future psychoanalytic perspectives as any detailed speculations about the old and tired instinctual dialectics of male-female biology.

Employment of the notion of sexual determinism in psychological studies of the human being, finally, strikes a callous and dehumanized note. It contracts the viewable focus of psychological processes and patterns to their secondary results in id impulse. Not that biology is not within the environment of human psyche — naturally, it is — but that human psyche cannot be flattened into nothing but reflections of its biological and social environment. This proposition appears to be self-evident; it has the logical support of earlier psychoanalytic practice. For if no distinction could be made between the environment and the environed, there would be no point to the principle that impulse determines psyche or that culture conditions it. And individual psyche — in this case, the environed — may have qualities and meanings relevant to it and it alone, even though it requires special environments in which to unfold. But it is not the same as its environment of biology or society. Without the validity of this distinction, the whole psychoanalytic enterprise — indeed, the whole field of psychology itself — would fold like an accordian from both sides.

Among the great equalizers of our time, inevitably forcing

biological and sociological models of therapy into the background, are atomic energy and automation, birth control pills and the population explosion, walks in outer space and instant electronic communication, rising economic and cultural expectations. Their possible future literally staggers the metapsychological imagination. Pro or con, no psychoanalytic perspective can remain unaffected by them; no one listening to radio, watching television or reading the daily press can. But tuned in or out, everyone alive is being touched by these great changes in experience, knowledge and action. Let him whose ego is defended and interpersonal self secure tell where they are really heading. I doubt that anyone is defended and secure enough yet, because their implications continue to shake our experience from day to day in ways that obstruct our direct awareness of their meaning and order. For better or worse, these great changes will require a metapsychology of individual psyche that biological and sociological metapsychologists did not dream of, let alone cope with. In this perspective lies the future vision of a psychoanalytic philosophy equal to these great social, scientific and technological changes we are now living through. Every individual psyche in our time inevitably participates in that future.

Chapter 5

EVOLUTIONARY PSYCHOANALYTIC METAPSYCHOLOGY

IN support of the discussions in Chapters 1 and 3, it is useful to consider the influence of biological and social Darwinsim on id and ego-interpersonal psychoanalysis. The step is, after all, a short one from survival of the fittest to a destructive instinct or innate power drive, from these but another to a social jungle of persons with inborn animal motives — if, in truth, uniqueness of individual psyche is delusion — and from these again a short step to basing a whole social order upon them. That so-called psychological realism that simply asserts animal origins of human psyche and is done with it actually loses itself in fruitless and futile fantasy. For this is not realism but rationalization, looking at aggression and violence, war and genocide and, as profound tautology, rewording this barbarous social behavior as instinct for preservation of self and territory, sex and destruction, and so on. Why, if Darwinism is essentially an evolutionary perspective, ignore the possible emergence of qualitatively new and humanized consciousness? Why not make this the platform of a new psychological realism?

In general reviews of the subject, it is often said that psychoanalysis is being taught and practiced as a manipulative or management type of therapy. The sense in which this is generally true may, however, be broken down into two sorts of factors. These are: those arising from traditions and procedures of the biological and the sociological models and those arising from present social arrangements of the culture at large. While it is clear from this breakdown that any psychotherapy requires some metapsychology or other for human use at all, it is far from clear that psychoanalysis requires a manipulative metapsychology to demarcate its therapeutic inquiry. In any case, the manipulative requirement has yet to be demonstrated as necessary and beyond question. From this it follows that structure of psychoanalysis can also set its basic terms of therapeutic inquiry in accordance with free and open metapsychologies of humanism, science and democracy. But from this, in turn, a disturbing query also follows. If manipulation and management of patients is neither necessary nor beyond question, why, then, is it so firmly set in the two established psychoanalytic models? The common-sense answer to this is simply because psychoanalysts and patients bring such defense mechanisms and security operations to their collaborative experience of therapy.

Psychoanalytic coparticipants do not, as a rule, have to transcend the established beliefs, values and ideals in which they make and live their lives. Nor, indeed, are they ordinarily expected to strive to do so. Their id aims and ego-interpersonal aspirations are ordinarily no better or worse than those of the society and culture in which they undertake their therapeutic inquiries. Even that rare psychoanalyst with enough courage, imagination and high standard of psychological purpose to extend himself beyond established beliefs, values and ideals about adjustment and adaptation — as some, I believe, do — is still usually bound in the particular case because many patients strive to overcome id and ego-interpersonal patterns and problems that prevent their getting on with such beliefs, values and ideals. Yet psychoanalysts are generally prepared, however, to terminate therapy as patients adjust id and adapt ego-interpersonal relations at home and work and, more broadly, achieve a stable range of viable satisfactions and securities. To proceed from this, they would have to develop capacities for the genuine uniqueness of individuality and enjoy its direction and fulfillment, that also require enough courage, imagination and high standard of psychological purpose of that rare patient who extends himself beyond established adjustment and adaptation; again, I believe some do. At such points, both psychoanalyst and patient have to grasp and hold perspective and objectivity toward these very beliefs, values and ideals. They have to distinguish the customary from the reflective, the conventional from the immediate, the stereotyped from the insightful in their daily experience of living.*

---

*For this distinction, see Dewey, J., and Tuft, J.: *Ethics,* 2nd ed. New York, Holt, 1932, chapter 9. This is Dewey's clearest statement of the individual and social origins of

The special sense in which id and ego-interpersonal therapies are manipulative may now be stated as a series of direct propositions. Psychoanalytic coparticipants in these fields of therapy are usually well-acculturated — if, in some ways, not particularly adjusted or adapted — members of their society. They live in institutional arrangements and work through beliefs, values and ideals that are material and synthetic, aggressive and competitive. In id and ego-interpersonal psychoanalysis, they do not ordinarily transcend the cultural aspirations of their social environment, either. Outcomes of these models of therapy are largely material and synthetic, aggressive and competitive, QED.

While practicing psychoanalysts may find it difficult to predict when and how this can change, or even if it ever will, they do not, of course, have to do this in order to practice psychoanalysis well. For the present, they may nonetheless probe to discover how deeply their selected model of therapy is rooted in the prevailing social arrangements and established beliefs, values and ideals. If they do not actually succeed in disentangling one from the other, they may then better appreciate where practice of psychoanalytic psychology ends and field work of cultural anthropology begins. And they may better distinguish processes and patterns studied in psychoanalytic structure, as well, from beliefs, values and ideals held in psychoanalytic metapsychology with a patient. This occurs because they happen to be who they are at that time, in that place, during that experience of therapy. But in order to distinguish them, psychoanalysts need a conscious judgment of the relation of psychology to both biology and sociology, which workers in both id and ego-interpersonal psychoanalysis have so far done most to clarify. They also need a conscious estimate of the critical omission of both these models, and to this I now turn.

At present, only infrequently and with difficulty do psychoanalytic coparticipants get beyond the two categories of human experience that Sullivan, for example, calls satisfaction and security. In clinical inquiry, his empirical focus does not, of

---

standards of moral activity. In his later *Theory of Valuation* (Chicago, University of Chicago, 1938), he emphasizes social origins. By then, he is more interested in biosocial conditions of change, however, than in the psychological origins of insight and responsibility guiding it. In "Dewey's Theory of Human Nature," (*Psychiatry*, 12:77-85, 1949) I review this varying emphasis in his work.

course, differ from that of his colleagues in ego psychology, except as discussed in Chapter 3, for terminology and perspective. He would satisfy needs, they, id impulses; he would maintain the interpersonal self's security operations, they, the ego's mechanisms of defense. Astute clinician though he undoubtedly was, he did not build the theory to see patients desirous or capable of further psychological objectives and therefore did not look for therapeutic significance in human pursuits other than satisfaction and security.

His view here, as that of most contemporary workers, follows the principle of unity of theory and practice. It is also possible to present it from the other side, namely that he did not look for therapeutic significance in human pursuits other than satisfaction and security and therefore did not build the theory to see patients desirous or capable of further psychological objectives. Spelled out from the systematic side of theory or the clinical side of practice, his view, however, remains essentially the same. Its internal logic is good and sound. But it may be another case of logic having to give way to experience. Consider but one aspect of it. When Sullivan denies the actual experience of personal uniqueness in terms of previous commitments to a point of view, he commits the idealistic fallacy. For when he adopts this idea as part of a system of ideas and direct inquiry fails to confirm the idea, he cannot then use it to deny existence to anything in actual fact without grossly distorting both inquiry and fact. Perhaps he thought patients (and psychoanalysts?) too disturbed, their social order too distorted, psychological change too difficult. These and other conjectures may be set forth to account for his rather stark view of genuine individuality of the psyche. Whatever his reason for doing it, he went as far as possible, however, to eliminate it. Because he would not claim to know anything without observing it and because he could not observe its patterned recurrence, he excluded it from any future scientific psychiatry. As though this were not put strongly enough, he even thought of its reported experience as evidence for psychiatric illness, diagnosing it a delusion.

How Sullivan defends this hard diagnosis is of some interest in this connection, as well as in its own right, as a mistaking of his own criterion of relevance for interpersonal theory. His purpose is served, he writes, "if it warns anyone that I never expect to know all about his personality."* In line with this criterion, however, he may either accept individuality even though no one ever expects to know all about his own or anyone else's or, no matter why he rejects it, also reject satisfaction and security for that same reason. If it is possible to know something about individuality, as it is to know something about satisfaction and security (which, of course, does not mean knowing all about any of the three) then if it is plausible to discard one as delusion, it appears equally plausible to discard the other two on this same ground. As long as limited knowledge does not suffice in one case, on what grounds can it do so in the other two? Granted, even, that the experience of personal uniqueness is itself a truly singular, nonrecurring event, what becomes of that actual occurrence and its later consequences? Though deeply committed to the cultural and interpersonal perspective, he did not, curiously enough, detect signs of established beliefs, values and ideals cutting into his conceptual vision when he "inveighed against the 'delusion of unique individuality.' " But his is not the only expression of this view.

From earliest beginnings, psychoanalysts have tacitly employed various forms of Darwinism as the philosophies in which to state and support id and ego-interpersonal metapsychologies. The interpretive power of Darwinism for mass culture today is practically beyond question in military, industrial and political affairs, and its use as justification of psychoanalytic perspectives is practially unconscious. The impact of inherited tradition on actual observation, as both aid and hindrance, is a very old story in all science, art and philosophy. It has yet to be told, however, about the impact of Darwinism on personal uniqueness in psychiatry, human psyche in psychoanalysis and individuality in psychology. Within the limited scope of this chapter, I review some highlights of only a small part of the story.

Like most students of Freud's writings, I, too, once accepted at face value his own estimate that he did for psychology what Darwin had previously done for biology. He pronounced it "a psychological blow to man's narcissism and compared it with the

---

*Sullivan, H.: *Conceptions of Modern Psychiatry.* Washington, W. A. White Psychiatric Foundation, 1947, p. vi; italics omitted.

biological blow delivered by the theory of descent and the earlier cosmological blow aimed at it by the discovery of Copernicus."* And "theory of descent," of course, refers to Darwin's work. But consider here that a contributor to science is not always best situated in historical relation to the results of his effort to evaluate their enduring significance. Those who later pursue problems he opens up, regardless of their perspectives and procedures, are as bound to the climates of opinion and conditions of thought in which they live and work, moreover, as he was to his. This makes it possible, from our vantage point, to place Freud's biological model far closer to Darwinism than he originally did. Paraphrasing the above quotation from his papers, it is then Darwinian biology that actually delivered a revolutionary approach to the study of human species and, in the process, human psyche as well. From this point of view, because the burden of id metapsychology derives from evolutionary biology, the first model of psychoanalysis may instead be considered a trial effort to revive and legitimate direct study of the human psyche in this post-1859 Darwinian era.

Even the chosen and most sympathetic of Freud's biographers cannot understand why, in spite of Darwin's obvious and enduring influence, Freud seems pointedly to avoid crediting his views (for example, of self-preservation and natural selection) in his own metapsychology of early childhood experience. Jones actually calls it "an extraordinary part of the story . . . a baffling problem"† in his discussion of this development of ideas in relation to personality. He finally fails to discover why Freud does not admit to being as fully Darwinian as he deeply was and would direct attention to his personal psychology for the answer. Such is the problem of his biographers, as well as psychoanalysts of history or historians of psychoanalysis, sympathetic or not, but it need not deflect critical psychoanalysts who would acknowledge

---

*Freud, S.: Resistances to psychoanalysis, In *Collected Papers*. London, Hogarth, 1950, vol. 5, p. 173; italics omitted.

†Jones, E.: *The Life and Work of Sigmund Freud*. New York, Basic Books, 1957, vol. 3, p. 310. A central aspect of this "baffling problem," accordingly, is Freud's long-expressed preference for Lamarck's theory of inheritance of acquired characteristics in the face of all the best evidence against it.

the pervasive influence of biological and social categories of evolution in id and ego-interpersonal psychoanalysis; nor, indeed, prevent them from distinguishing a contributor's personal biography from his empirical and systematic work and both, again, from the later reconstruction of others. Since the plan of this study, however, does not include tracing and documenting the influence of biological and social Darwinism on psychoanalytic theory and therapy, I refer the interested reader to other sources.*

Present students of Freud's work are not, in any case, bound to his interpretation of it. They are free to make their own, as well. Suffice it to say, for the context of this study, that Jones's "baffling problem" shrinks from systematic and structural to merely private and biographical significance when compared with the heavy influence of evolutionary biology on formulations of all instinct theories. This, in turn, is compatible with the judgment of Darwin's influence as fundamental to the origins of psycho-analysis. Some factors in this judgment are as follows: first, Darwin's was by far the dominant theory of evolution in the latter half of the nineteenth century; second, Freud's failure to credit it does not actually exclude the possibility that Darwin's work deeply influenced him; and third, the contributions of both may, in retrospect, be seen as having fused biology and psychology into a common-sense core of beliefs, values and ideals that still nurtures the conventional wisdom justifying both id and ego-interpersonal psychoanalysis.

It is nevertheless still true that Freud did not often relate his basic assumptions about human psyche to the great historical and evolutionary movements of thought in nineteenth-century anthropology broadly conceived, among whose leaders Darwin is

---

*For example, Dewey, J.: *The Influence of Darwin on Philosophy*. New York, Holt, 1910; Hofstadter, R.: *Social Darwinism in American Thought*. Philadelphia. University of Pennsylvania, 1944, Murphy, G.: *Personality*. New York, Harper, 1947; and Schneider, H.: *A History of American Philosophy*. New York, Columbia University, 1946, chapter 31 to chapter 33, entitles "Speculative Biology," "Evolutionary Theology," and "Genetic Social Philosophy."

Together with major statements of id and ego-interpersonal psychoanalysis, these works provide ample materials for exploring various aspects of biological and social Darwinism in both models of psychoanalytic therapy. To my knowledge, no single work is devoted to it.

undoubtedly front rank. To appreciate Darwin's fundamental influence on id metapsychology, on the other hand, does not at all detract from appreciating the original value of Freud's development of the biological model of psychoanalysis. The principles of self-preservation and self-assertiveness, for example, are enduring effects of that influence in both id and ego-interpersonal perspectives. These principles are, of course, clearly evident in the first model of therapy. But beyond Darwin's peerless dominance in biology, as his evolutionary theory began to dominate sociology, they also began to appear in the second model of therapy. It is, in short, a matter of historical record that Darwinism spurred the reconstruction of perspectives on all human sciences and even religion.

A few chapters of post-Darwinian thought, therefore, provide a good introduction of this radical change of climate of opinion and inquiry.* They also suggest why the psychoanalysis of instinct adjustment and defense adaptation struck such strong roots so deeply in American culture. But consider further this easy and quick reception of both evolutionary biology and id psychoanalysis, for it points up their intimate relation indirectly. Freud, it is well known, expressed profound misgivings about the American way of life and even about his own possible wide acceptance by it. Was he, however, aware that the cultural milieu of rugged materialism and frontier philosophy, so warmly hospitable to his own various instinct theories, had already been rationalized by appeal to Darwin's evolutionary and biosocial principles of struggle for survival and natural selection, utilitarian aggression and self-assertiveness? Or that by the 1880's here, the relation of instinct to intelligence was already a major topic of inquiry and speculation? Or that, more generally, late nineteenth-century American thought in natural and social science, in moral and religious philosophy, had warmly received and widely applied the evolutionary hypothesis long before the birth of psychoanalysis in Vienna? Instinctual and evolutionary biology was to exert no greater influence on id psychoanalysis than it had, in fact, already exerted on American thought. It is in this light difficult to

---

*See previous footnote.

see how anyone could express profound misgivings about possible wide acceptance of psychoanalysis anywhere without also having similar misgivings about the biological model itself.

It is against the background of evolutionary biology that the first model of psychoanalysis, then, establishes the primacy of instincts for interpretive therapeutic work. This, of course, is the basic category of id impulse that by psychosexuality extends beyond biological instincts into the second category of mechanisms of ego defense; in interpersonal terms, the basic category of need satisfaction that, by mind-body continuity, extends beyond energy transformations into the second category of operations for self security. But in either terminology, the relation between the two categories remains vague. Interpersonal psychoanalysts do not further clarify this continuity of mind and body, while id and ego psychoanalysts cannot locate ego psychology in id biology no matter how hard they stretch psychosexuality beyond its early reliance on physiological excitation. Some stretch so hard that by the late 1930's, they finally sever ego from id and attribute to it autonomous functions similar to those of the interpersonal self. It is this very same instinctual and evolutionary biology of id psychoanalysis, worked into beliefs, values and ideals of social experience, that remains Darwin's lasting influence on ego-interpersonal psychoanalysis, as well.

Neither id nor ego-interpersonal psychoanalysts, however, move beyond these two categories of id or need satisfaction and ego-interpersonal defense or security to still a third of individual psyche and its direction. Consider, for example, the therapies of Anna Freud and Reich. Both are split-level models in the special sense that in Anna Freud's terms transference of ego defense lacks systematic connections with transference of id impulse and, in his metaphor, a many-sided character armor is fitted over libidinal strivings from the outside. Perhaps they were working too closely in time and place to Freud and his revised definition of anxiety to appreciate its implications in full. They did not realize that transference of id, or in Sullivan's terms, need satisfaction, could no longer be the first and primary category and by itself would never again guide the interpretation and support the outcome of psychoanalytic therapy. In this respect, their models, however, are based in id and ego-interpersonal Darwinism.

With the definition of anxiety revised, Freud and his followers could have changed the future course of psychoanalysis as inquiry and experience. The new definition itself implicitly admits the failure of evolutionary biology and, by the same token, the failure of the biological model for further constructions of psychoanalytic psychology. But it took nearly fifteen years for others to extend this model beyond the pleasure principle and in order to study character armor, ego defense mechanism or interpersonal security operation, set forth the sociological model. During this period, it should be emphasized, no one using the perspective of id metapsychology — neither S. Freud and Reich, for example, nor Anna Freud and Hartmann — pushed the relation of ego anxiety to defense mechanism any further than Sullivan moved the relation of interpersonal anxiety to security operation. Among contributors to this second model, many differences in terminology, patient population, philosophy of science, cultural tradition and social background are no less strikingly evident than, indeed, their many differences in psychology and metapsychology.

All such differences wear thin, however, compared with the large blind spot ego-interpersonal psychoanalysts share among themselves and with their predecessors, the id psychoanalysts. They fail to create substantive leverage in theory for erasing manipulative factors from their perspectives on psychoanalysis and therefore do not create it in therapeutic practice. This leverage would derive from adding a third category of psychology of self-directive individuality to the established categories of biology of id impulse and sociology of ego-interpersonal relation. It suffices at this point to note that interpretive perspectives of psychoanalysis developed from biology to sociology to psychology. In Chapter 6, I discuss this third category in relation to experience and behavior and in Chapter 8, the psychological model it demarcates.

In the first and second models, psychoanalysts set out to accomplish the goals patients and their common social order put to them. First, id psychoanalysts liberate libido through genetic resolution of early childhood conflict; second, ego-interpersonal psychoanalysts reshape the adaptive structure and redirect the function of ego defenses or interpersonal securities. By seeking and accomplishing these goals, they tightly circumscribe the ordering of personal fulfillment, however, with the conventional wisdom of established beliefs, values and ideals. It is this tightness that may well account for the growing interest of some psychoanalysts and patients in extrasensory perception, telepathy in transference, mysticism and the occult, and so on.

Perhaps so termed in order to avoid responsibility for scientific description, these interests actually reflect strong evidence for the facing of fears and loosening of repressions on a very large cultural scale. The uncritical and unconscious acceptance of Darwinism narrows down the individual's vision of his psyche and, of course, its range of development, to satisfying id impulse and defending ego-interpersonal security. As a matter of good therapeutic procedure, it is then necessary to reduce, inhibit and redefine other significant dimensions of experience in accordance with these two and if that is not possible, treat them as distorted and delusional. In setting these goals, id and ego-interpersonal psychoanalysts try to answer the demands of the social order by influencing their patients to answer them. And patients undertaking psychoanalysis practiced in accordance with these models, it turns out, also seek to answer the demands of their social order by accepting the influence of their psychoanalysts. The same, of course, holds true for all adjustive and adaptive psychotherapies.

Ordinarily, no psychoanalyst and patient need be overly concerned about being able to do this, for it signifies adjustment and adaptation to their biological, social and ego-interpersonal environment. If they also remain unaware of having to do this, they may at least get on with it and hope for the best possible adjustment and adaptation. But this, they may respond, is the way things really are in the life of a species primarily involved with satisfying id impulses and defending ego-interpersonal securities. Therefore, they continue, psychoanalyst and patient may justifiably work toward these id and ego-interpersonal ends; for pursuing the right means and securing the desired ends are themselves surely no small and easy tasks. Patients who become better socialized and acculturated, they conclude, also gain a certain measure of self-respect.

Ego-interpersonal psychoanalysts make this point in the various languages of ego strength and competence, esteem and regard for self. While larger self-respect is both desired and desirable, its ego-interpersonal meaning has yet to be adequately spelled out. Without a third category of individual psyche and personal fulfillment, in whose view does the patient gain self-respect? His society's, his peers's, his own? And what is the basis for differentiating among them? The general answer is, since the original lack arises through interaction with significant others, it may also be overcome in that same context. Adopting this perspective, ego-interpersonal therapy is remarkably consistent about ego strength and competence or esteem and regard for self. These are lost and found in social and ego-interpersonal experience. In the context of Darwinism, the psychoanalytic ego-interperson may be seen as a social and cultural system of reflected responses maintaining itself somewhere between the organism and its environment. It is essentially a constellation of patterns of events external to the psyche. The notion of self-respect may, in this way, acquire some special meaning as psychoanalytic sociology. But without a direct reference to individual and personal psyche, it has no logical or psychological means here to distinguish a persona from its bearer, a fictive facade from its author, a social self from its maker or an ego-interpersonal self from the individual's relation to it.

The outcome of the biological and sociological models, therefore, is reorganization of attitude and behavior in accordance with rebuilt defense and security operations, renovated goals and controls. These evolutionary therapies and their variations are then not merely manipulative. More justly than in jest, they may be termed new secular religiosities of adjustment and adaptation whose practice is not psychological and individuating but biosocial and valuational. Take Sullivan, for example. In the regular format of id and ego-interpersonal Darwinism, he emphasizes biological needs for sleep, rest, shelter, clothing, food, drink and lust, together with social securities pertaining to the evolution of interpersonal self. But as already discussed, he appraises the individual's personal uniqueness as having no point of interest other than psychiatric disturbance. Nor, of course, does he even find it necessary to demonstrate in either interpersonal psychiatry or social experience that individual psyche has no therapeutic significance. He may essentially assert it because it does not characterize his emphasis alone. It characterizes all psychotherapies that focus on the two categories of id or need satisfaction and defense mechanism or security operation and do not integrate this third category of individual psyche and its direction.

The psychology of individuality in shared experience provides for a new model of psychoanalytic therapy. The immediate focus of its development in this study is, however, to explore whether psychoanalysis is more than a manipulative therapy. While it may be widely practiced in this way, it does not automatically follow that it can be practiced in no other. It may, of course, also be done in a free, open and exploratory perspective, as well. Besides this point in principle, there are clinical factors to be considered. For some time, patients whose needs seem reasonably satisfied and securities reasonably defended — in accordance, respectively, with biology of id impulse and sociology of ego-interpersonal relation — have been undertaking psychoanalysis because they report they are anxious and depressed and feel miserable. The distinct contributions of these two metapsychologies, for them, are very soon exhausted as guidelines to further therapeutic inquiry into their psychological problems. Since they fail, moreover, to resolve their problems primarily in biological, social or ego-interpersonal terms, their psychoanalyst has to be prepared for another kind of psychoanalytic experience. No longer can he act the id mirror or ego-interpersonal expert; he has to prepare for direct individualized participation in long-term therapeutic inquiry instead, as free of impersonal experience about his patient and himself as both can make it.

In this light, certain issues in current theory and practice have to be reformulated for the study of human psyche in psychoanalysis. Required here are analyses of issues interfering with this study and hypotheses to modify them. To meet this requirement, I have presented historical and critical factors in the first five chapters to show why the biological and sociological models do not treat individual psyche in its own terms. In the following chapters, I develop some implications of adding this third category of individual psyche to the two categories of id or need satisfaction and ego defense or interpersonal security already established.

Chapter 6

EXPERIENCE, BEHAVIOR AND
INDIVIDUAL PSYCHE

PSYCHOANALYSIS is undergoing a thorough reappraisal of the relations of its theory and practice. No interpretation of metapsychology, no study of theory, no report of therapy is done until its author presents the credentials of instinctual dialectics, struggle for power, collective unconscious, pure will and so on. For his part, the reader is well-conditioned and quickly recognizes the stamp of Freud, Adler, Jung or Rank. In actual psychoanalytic therapy, the objective is not often identified, however, as the patient's desire to know how inner psychic experience extends into outward social and ego-interpersonal behavior. For though the bridge between the two is usually distorted, disturbed and difficult to make out, its existence is not, therefore, beyond reflection.

Throughout most psychological inquiry, this bridge between experience and behavior is simply used as an unexamined belief of immediate experience. Yet both psychoanalyst and patient at times are aware that they need clearer perception of its structure, more reliable understanding of its origin and a better grasp of its distinct possibilities for change in order to sustain their inquiry. They become aware of such needs without interpretive meta-psychology to alert them but simply because they meet in the experiential field of therapy. This, of course, suffices to account for their working at it, namely that a competent psychoanalyst undertakes continous and long-term inquiry into problems a suffering patient cannot resolve on his own.

It is only in the search for metapsychology to interpret how or why this bridge joins the individual and psychic to the biosocial and ego-interpersonal that serious confusion arises. Where it is not accepted as a matter of immediate experience, conscious efforts have to be made to establish it in the transference and resistance of id impulse and ego-interpersonal relation. These efforts, however, do not prove successful, mainly because these biological and sociological foundations are off psychological center and lean too far over on the environmental side. While the bridge relating experience to behavior, then, may be clear in fact, it tends to become confusing in interpretation; and I do not plan here to propose still another. The important source of confusion, I propose instead, is a solid yet uncritical reliance on biological and sociological perspectives in psychoanalysis whose current reality as therapeutic inquiry is already moving in new directions.

The currently confusing relation of experience to behavior may therefore be directly attributed to this negative diagnosis of individual psyche and, as a consequence, its dissociation from the realistic and proper domain of psychoanalytic therapy. But such negative diagnosis is not a recent innovation of ego-interpersonal therapy; its origins stretch back to the early beginnings of id therapy. As one major result, psychoanalysis now has the wide and unfortunate reputation of being a method of adjustment and adaptation, a therapy of gaining approval and success in terms of the established beliefs, values and ideals of a given social and cultural environment without due regard for their psychological merits.

As a further result, other psychotherapies obviously influenced by these estimable goals of adjustment and adaptation are developing short-term procedures to attain these very same goals more directly, rapidly and efficiently. Patients and others in psychological trouble are generally aware of this state of affairs. Some reject psychoanalysis in favor of less intensive psychotherapies in order to adapt their behavior more quickly to the material and competitive struggles for survival, safety and comfort. Others do not consider psychoanalysis a therapy of choice because they are not so anxious and distorted as to prevent their preparing a personality for approved, adaptive and rewarding transaction on their own. Still others do not consider psychoanalysis a therapy of need until they begin to show disruptive psychotic signs or visible suicidal impulses and are then influenced to seek it. There is also that small fanatic minority that would reject intensive psychoanalytic therapy under any circumstances. In short, serious psychoanalysts are up against limitations in both id and ego-interpersonal therapy, and troubled patients face precisely these same limitations whether they choose psychoanalytic or other psychotherapies or, no matter how troubled, try to make it on their own. Even those who reject psychoanalysis, however, are also struggling in some sense — perhaps, unaware — to overcome the limitations of id and ego-interpersonal Darwinism written large across the conventional wisdom of the culture.

In any psychotherapy, the problem of manipulation is subordinate to theory of motivation. Reinforcement theory, for example, depends on the use of compulsion and coercion in various forms. Its very name suggests the use of power, its controlling overtone is unmistakable. The same may be said for forces of faculty psychology, instinctual drives of the id and ego-interpersonal power motives. But therapeutic manipulation deriving from theory of motivation cannot be readily depicted within the working conditions of psychoanalytic inquiry. For in that inquiry, nothing significant can be said about the motivation of beliefs, values and ideals at the first four orders of (1) observation, (2) definition, (3) postulation and (4) theory.

But in the overall structure of psychoanalysis, the close relation of manipulation and motivation extends beyond empirical and systematic inquiry into perspectives on (5) metapsychology, most generally into philosophies of life. It extends, that is, into matters of social organization, political arrangements, economic realities and institutionalized patterns forming and being formed within the culture. Pro or con, it nevertheless exists to be dealt with, and to this essential fact of life all motivation theories and manipulative therapies finally fall back in order to support selected patterns of experience and behavior that the motivators and manipulators believe are good for themselves and therefore good for their patients. They do indeed have moments of objectivity in which they judge something good and valuable, irrespective of the immediate requirements of adjustment and adaptation. For being alive, they must always take one or another attitude — if only that of neutrality — toward the liberating and distorting effects of established beliefs, values and ideals on psychic function. But this, too, at some point involves a moral judgment of their moral power. Inevitably, it is metapsychology. In any case, every psychoanalyst is a metapsychologist at least to that extent, no more, no less than every other psychotherapist and every other researcher in human psychology.

Theory of motivation has as long a history as Western thought itself. Coherent formulations may be traced from ancient Hebrew prophets, Greek thinkers and medieval theologians and philosophers through the associationists and structuralists and, especially since Darwin's great influence, from the instinct and drive theorists of the last century to the animal reinforcement experimenters and cognitive theorists in our own time. In early psychoanalysis, Freud and his followers continually faced the problem of doing justice to the psychology of transference, resistance, anxiety and unconscious experience, which they studied in spite of severe limitations imposed by their biological bias in metapsychology. But even behaviorists using reinforcement theory in apparently value-free experiments with animals have yet to apply their results to significant motives and attitudes that men relate to themselves and others. They have yet to extend reinforcement theory, above all, to the direct psychological study of motives and attitudes as constituted and experienced outside awareness.

The problem of unconscious motivation is still crucial for metapsychologies of psychoanalysis and psychotherapy. It is in this connection that practicing psychoanalysts are often disappointed with the curt way in which behaviorists dismiss dynamic psychology. This, however, is not surprising because behaviorists usually oppose the notion of reinforcement to that of human experience. They first distinguish experience from behavior, then exclude the former in favor of the latter, and finally cannot make motivational sense of either the present conscious experience of beliefs, values and ideals or the past experience of those still being unconsciously sought in the present. In effect, they set motive apart from experience and acknowledge its existence only as they can reconstrue it as reinforcible behavior. By way of analogy, it is fair to say, they throw the nineteenth-century forces and faculties of psychology out the back window only to welcome them back through the front door as twentieth-century drives and reinforcers of behavior.

The limitations of a behaviorist view of dynamic psychotherapy are well known. They derive from established canons of behaviorism that essentially make human experience an inadmissible construct on the critical ground that its processes and patterns are mentalistic. According to the hard behaviorist line, the notion of human experience "cannot be invoked to lend ancillary validity to a construct that is otherwise anchored in behavioral phenomena. Because its reference is outside the theory, introducing it does nothing to bind together the structure of the theory."* As one expected result, the bulk of this work is then devoted to theories, methods and findings of laboratory experiments with infrahuman species — cats and dogs, mice and rats. For such animal studies, any human experience is considered irrelevant not just as construct but because of possible anthropomorphic projection, also in fact.

In this way, hard-line behaviorism excludes from the structure of psychological science all sorts of relatedness and communication covered by the notion of human experience in all the psychotherapies. Taken to a logical but hopefully unacceptable conclusion, it makes studies of human psyche and its pathologies somehow disappear from the domain of science by referring human experience outside behaviorist theory. Although the relations of experience and behavior may be difficult, they are at present critical for contemporary philosophy of psychology and psychoanalysis, and they will not be soon resolved or easily stated. But studies of human psyche and its pathologies, it should be noted, do not seem to be fading away either, at any rate, not simply by manipulating this major distinction of experience from behavior.

Why there is this methodological impasse and how to master it are not simple questions, however. Even a brief review of nineteenth-century origins of biological metapsychologies would indicate that the conceptual relations of experience and behavior become increasingly strained from 1859 onward. After instinct

---

*Bolles, R.: *Theory of Motivation.* New York, Harper & Row, 1967, page 17. For further discussion of this theme, see my review in *American Journal of Psychotherapy,* *22*:105-107, 1968.

and drive theorists whole-heartedly adapt the implications of evolutionary biology to studies of the human organism, they extend its then long overdue Darwinist emphasis on animal behavior. But if this is so, any enduring change in their relations depends on creating a rationale for the following three major categories peculiar to the experience of human species — id or need satisfaction, social and ego-interpersonal security, individuality and its direction — without the currently undue emphasis on animal behavior. Contemporary psychology and psychoanalysis would benefit from this change, but it is clear they are not about to make it.

Hard-line behaviorism is usually set forth as the complementary but unreachable opposite of hard-line experientialism, and the dispute is not being resolved in the language and thought of current controversy.* The line between experience and behavior continues to harden from both sides and therefore keeps them so far apart because the dispute probably cuts far deeper into basic presuppositions about their relations than previously suggested in public discussion. For these presuppositions are being articulated, pro and con, in the terms and perspectives of biological, social and ego-interpersonal Darwinism. Without going beyond them, it is not reasonable to expect distinctly human experience and generally animal behavior to have constructive relations in the near future. And if this were not so, the hope of ever getting beyond this impasse would be very slim, indeed.

The notion of human experience and the observation and definition of its coordinate terms, meanwhile, are both very much a part of psychoanalysis today, and the field of inquiry it designates is not about to disappear. Neither the notion, nor the observation and definition, nor the field of inquiry itself can abide by principles of behaviorism that strictly preclude reference to them. Practicing psychoanalysts continue to treat human beings who still experience themselves in distortion, disturbance and difficulty, and who then emit behaviors on the basis of this experience to the point of engaging a psychoanalyst and undergoing therapeutic inquiry. During these therapeutic inquiries,

*See Wann, T. (Ed.): *Behaviorism and Phenomenology.* Chicago, University of Chicago, 1964.

they still continue to use whatever structures of (1) observation, (2) definition, (3) postulation, (4) theory and (5) metapsychology they find most appropriate for their particular fields of experience.

At some future date, a mutually modified experiential-behavioral reconstruction may be worked out, probably in other terms and definitely with other presuppositions, and then be applied to such fields of inquiry as psychoanalysis. If this reconstruction is to be useful, it will have to modify the limits of biological, social and ego-interpersonal Darwinism or supplement its perspectives. A reconstruction of experience and behavior, however, is made more probable by the fact that neither can persevere without at some point also referring to the other. Only as the influence of Darwin's *Origin of Species* changes can the hard line dividing the two give way to a unified perspective on human living of individuals who feel, think, innovate, reorganize or at the risk of behaviorist disapproval, even experience. For if the two are so sharply set off from each other, how do they get back together again in a single affective and cognitive continuum? How is experience behaved, behavior experienced? Anyone who appraises and applies knowledge in his clinical and laboratory studies, even in his personal experience of his own social and cultural behavior, cannot deal seriously with these questions without first considering whether behavior is no less a function of experience than experience is a function of behavior. For behavior without experience becomes empty and, therefore, mechanical; experience without behavior becomes blind and, therefore, imprisoned. A program of psychoanalytic theory, therapy and research has to modify its original perspectives in order to face these vital considerations.

In line with this, a prevailing ambiguity in current psychoanalytic practice arises from the fact that in mirror procedure, a patient is no more supposed to know his psychoanalyst's metapsychology throughout than a psychoanalyst in active procedure knows his patient's even initially. It is an ambiguity of indefinite commitment about these biological, social, cultural, ego-interpersonal and psychological issues, and it points up how difficult it really is for any two coparticipants to know what their shared experience will become until they actually have it. This has been true of psychoanalytic therapy from its origins in hypnotic, cathartic and pressure procedures through its evolution into the id and ego-interpersonal models; but a historical review is not particularly helpful here. This ambiguity may be directly confronted, instead. If the psychoanalyst adopts the role of agent for certain beliefs, values and ideals rather than others, then his patient may wish to hear that directly stated at certain points in their collaborative effort. Or do they work together, as well, to enable the patient to grasp and extend his sense of individuality? Then this, too, he may wish to have clarified. It may be assumed that as a matter of decent procedure, he will also have the room to explore any established belief, value or ideal in order to clarify his own relation to it. Such statements and clarifications do not automatically erase the ambiguity of indefinite commitment; they only make it easier to study its consequences more directly.

If this ambiguity remains unnoticed on the outside fringes of therapeutic inquiry, the experience tends to unfold into interlocking transference and countertransference, resistance and counterresistance, anxiety and counteranxiety, and so on. It seems to become unaccountably involved in recurrent interlocking experiences. Even without judging the relative merits of the id, ego-interpersonal and psychic issues, if psychoanalyst and patient can consistently take one or another perspective, they may hope to get through these blockages. But if they alternate or hedge their views, they risk playing off any one against the others. When, for example, a patient criticizes some established belief, value or ideal, he may be reminded of still another he ignores; if he criticizes a biosocial or ego-interpersonal attitude, he may be reminded of his individual psyche; if he declares his personal self, he may be reminded of his relation to biosocial and ego-interpersonal attitudes; and if he affirms both, he may then be reminded of the animal origins of his biological nonself.

According to the conventional wisdom, man is a unified entity and possesses a total personality in which biological, social, cultural, ego-interpersonal and psychic categories intertwine from a holistic point of view. But the science and philosophy of their intertwined nature, today, are by no means capable of explicit determination, so that the notion of a unified or total personality is now essentially metaphor. If, in spite of deep gaps in knowledge, a particular psychoanalyst would avoid endless and repetitive interlocks with his patient who, if anxious and alert as though guided by unconscious radar sensitivity, could turn them into secure defenses against therapeutic movement, he still has another alternative open. He may find it useful to stand clear on some such issue in accordance with his perspective on metapsychology and do so simply as a matter of stating his own affirmed belief, judged value or cherished ideal.

Reconsider now the point of this brief digression. In practice of psychoanalysis with patients who are looking more inward for deeper understanding of their psychic resources — for, in graphic terms, a better map of their inner space — it is becoming more difficult for psychoanalysts to follow the outward id and ego-interpersonal metapsychologies and still sustain effective inquiry with these patients. If they do, something irreversible happens: The working inquiry breaks down, the therapeutic alliance dissolves, the experiential field of therapy splits, all under the pressure of conflict between inheritance and innovation. It is the ambiguity of indefinite commitment that arises here from a steady use of id and ego-interpersonal metapsychologies with patients who seek more genuine individuality in pursuit of personal fulfillment. And it is implicit in all the intricate, confusing divisions and reductions of human psyche into biological, social and ego-interpersonal terms. But metapsychology is not all.

In ongoing therapeutic inquiry, this ambiguity tends to mask the personal selves that psychoanalyst and patient actually possess and could otherwise attempt to define in their collaborative effort. Failure to notice the sense of personal self possessed by either coparticipant, of course, makes the experiential field appear psychologically vacant. That this vacancy usually is not openly acknowledged is quite to the point, for its tenants hide from each other behind all the ongoing concerns with biosocial patterns of id striving and ego-interpersonal security. Hidden from outward view, it is clear, are the ingoing concerns with individual psyche, inevitably the only source of innovative psychological change known to be reliable in any field of human experience, including that of therapy. Psychoanalyst and patient, together, may directly confront this ambiguity of their commitments with the shared aim of presenting them to each other and with a sense and definition of two personal selves openly committed to do the sharing. No longer need they limit inquiry to their me-you relations in the public ego-interpersonal mode; they may, in addition, now seek to extend themselves into I-thou relations in the private, personal mode.

If manipulative and management therapy, then, is the upshot of the biological and sociological models, it cuts a general edge of doubt around all such psychoanalytic interpretation to date. It reopens to question the place in human psychology of instinct and libido, force and drive, and all the other important id or need derivatives. It also reopens important questions about the meaning for human psyche of ego-interpersonal anxiety interpreted by myths and symbols of existentialism or described as scientific physiology of tissues and glands. It raises further questions, as well, about the meaning for individual psyche of ego-interpersonal defense and security interpreted by myths and symbols of corporate business culture or described as scientific sociology of approved and disapproved behavior. In the light of all this, some established modes of psychoanalytic interpretation have to be viewed as so much professional hocus-pocus, conferring irrational power and authority on the id and ego-interpersonal experts at adjustment and adaptation, as it ordinarily does in our conventional wisdom, and cloaking their judgments of behavior with a mystique of religious crisis, pure science or efficient procedure.

The newer varieties of behavior therapy, it should be noted, are no exceptions in this regard. They closely resemble in both methods and goals — though not in psychology and meta-psychology — the older prepsychoanalytic therapies of hypnosis, direct suggestion and catharsis. The ability to modify and remove behavior symptoms is estimable therapy and, in its own right, still above criticism. But a change in symptoms does not necessarily involve changes in the psyche, and I discuss some aspects of this issue in Chapter 11.

It has yet to be demonstrated that behavior therapy can

actually support ostracism of individual unconscious experience studied in a psychoanalytic psychology so radically different from its own. The main virtue of behavior therapy, of course, is to attempt exactly what its name implies it does — modify behavior — and nothing else. But if this is all it attempts, it cannot succeed even at that, however, with a live human being in possession of the most rudimentary of personal selves. And this is its main defect. Relying on the status and prestige of exact, efficient laboratory science, it is a newer form of symptom therapy. It first narrows down inquiry to patterns of behavior, which are essentially defined as different from those of etiquette, mannerism and propriety; and then it uses direct suggestion so that patients emit the approved and extinguish the disapproved from among their conspicuous social behaviors. Yet the chief source of approval and disapproval they draw upon, following a strictly behaviorist view, is that very same conventional wisdom from which the earlier id and later ego-interpersonal therapies also draw their beliefs, values and ideals. In view of this convergence in perspective, further consideration of behavior therapy does not advance the theme of this chapter. Instead, I now consider other aspects of the ambiguity of indefinite commitment in the first two models of psychoanalysis.

As a mirror or professional expert, the psychoanalyst treats the effects of his therapeutic inquiry on his patient's personal psychology as matters of transference and resistance. He does this to further a basic, consistent concern with adjusting id needs and adapting ego-interpersonal relations. Avoiding direct involvement with his patient's psyche, he follows a map of average, expectable attitudes and behaviors (including the study of attitudes separates ego-interpersonal from behavior therapy) and would have the patient follow this map, as well. After reaching the expected and approved destinations of their therapeutic journey, although terminating, both probably continue to use it in daily life. For as the patient eventually masters it, he learns to do what his psychoanalytic expert in satisfactions and securities effectively influences him to learn, unwittingly perhaps, but no less factually. Without judging it as psychoanalysis or experience, however, both work toward increasing the constructive interplay of ego-

-interpersonal attitudes and social behaviors. In this way, again, perhaps unwittingly, they exercise uncritical validation and support of the average, expectable beliefs, values and ideals consensually approved in their environing culture.

But how uniform are these beliefs, values and ideals? How widely are they sought and lived in the culture at large? Or is something new, at present, happening to them? In response to rising affluence and the results of unprecedented technology, they are undergoing rapid and critical reconstruction, and if it ever was, it no longer is easy to discern and apply average, expectable standards to individual experience. Appeal to them as approved and consensually validated guidelines, in this circumstance, is simplistic and beside the point, for it promotes the empty myth and metaphor of cliché experience. That any average beliefs, values and ideals ever did exist as such or if they ever were so widely sought and lived is still open to serious question. I do not pursue this theme further here because it extends into cultural anthropology, ethical philosophy and history of ideas. It is not primarily psychoanalytic and does not require answers of the ego-interpersonal expert. But with attitude and behavior so much in flux, the psychoanalyst too, cannot avoid the ambiguity of his own making. Neither his patient's nor his own personal uniqueness — by his definition, delusional — is capable of sighting any new belief, value or ideal to which they might both consider new adaptation. Appealing outward to once expectable yet now changing social, ego-interpersonal attitudes and behaviors, instead, only compounds the ambiguity.

But how, in the adaptive view, does a patient learn to readapt? How does he accept any established perspective in the experiential field of therapy? The answer is, in effect, simply put to him as follows: Accept your ego-interpersonal psychoanalyst's influence and he will expertly guide you to improved — that is, better approved — attitudes and behaviors. But in terms of his own beliefs, values and ideals deriving from that same cultural environment, this professional expert discourages his patients from digging at their roots in personal psychology. If the ego-interpersonal patient does not then explore his unique psyche on his own, and since he is not encouraged to do so (his psychoanalyst, of course, lacks the category of individuality) there really is nowhere for him to turn but to the readjustment of behavior and readaptation of attitude. Assuming he can make himself look and behave better, he directs his attention to the repatterning of his outward appearance. From the perspective of ego-interpersonal metapsychology, no other aim is in view.

At this point, a clear extension of psychoanalytic perspectives is indicated. In order to seek and find definition of his emergent psyche, the patient requires a measure of courage, imagination and high psychological purpose. But to succeed in these efforts, he also needs a measure of freedom to let go, now and then, of some carefully selected attitudinal and behavioral moorings long enough to sense the pulse and rhythm of his unique psyche, and clearly enough to make a reading of its sense and direction. To this end (besides courage and imagination, high psychological purpose and freedom to experience) he needs to know the significance of his individuality for personal fulfillment; and this invariably requires that he learn to distinguish the psychic from the social as living qualities of experience. But if he cannot already do this, and if in id and ego-interpersonal therapy he is not encouraged toward it, the expert in adaptation helps him best with a reasonable facsimile of the real thing. For in biological and sociological models, it is absurd and delusional to value a high standard of psychological purpose for this human species whose members engage in daily battle to become best fitted to survive the competitive, predatory risks of a social and cultural jungle. Highest though this species may be on the evolutionary scale, it is unfortunately still judged animal.

In various contexts, I refer to this category of individual psyche and its direction as personal uniqueness, personal or psychic self, genuine individuality or individual psyche, and to its linkage with participation in shared experience. Through its development, the scientific, aesthetic and democratic ideals of truth, beauty and freedom are created, realized and enjoyed. These are inevitably constituents of the ideal good, no matter what else is found to constitute it. In this perspective, I treat individual psyche as the third category of psychoanalytic metapsychology, supplementing those of id impulse and ego-interpersonal relation. Why introduce it into established and evolving metapsychologies? The answer is simply to provide for a clear and explicit recognition of the individual's personal relation to his id, ego-interpersonal and social self. In this way, it is the main support of the psychological observation and definition of shared experience directly made within the actual field of therapy.

The relations of the psychic to both the biological and the social and ego-interpersonal are obviously not to be found in the biology and sociology of the ego-interpersonal self. Empirical and systematic statements about the one are not reducible to empirical and systematic statements about the others. Emanating from a genuine sense of individual psyche, the pursuit of personal fulfillment is a different mode of experience and with this third category added may be appreciated in its own psychoanalytic terms. It requires inclusion as unique subject matter; it cannot persist parceled out among others; certainly not among biology and sociology. For being individual, the psyche is therefore literally indivisible.

Although the experience of individual psyche does not fit into id and ego-interpersonal perspectives, as already indicated, it need not be analyzed as absurd fantasy or psychiatric delusion. The Darwinist framework itself is not absolute; nor, of course, are its implications. It may instead be so modified as to provide a basis in psychoanalytic therapy for the psychology of shared experience, supplementing both the biology of id impulse and the sociology of ego-interpersonal relation. But a curious thing happens to id impulse and ego-interpersonal relation when individual psyche is introduced as their supplement. What was once a passive and reducible datum, to be lost in the id or among reflected appraisals of ego-interpersonal others, now becomes the active and directive factor in personal experience, knowledge and appreciation of the other two. Reconstructing biological and sociological models in accordance with the psychology of shared experience, then, is not a simple addition to this third category but rather the dynamic transformation of relations among all three. In this transformation, it turns out, the sense of individuality and ordering of personal fulfillment that Darwinist biosocial builders fail to acknowledge in id and ego-interpersonal therapy becomes the psychological cornerstone of psychoanalytic inquiry and experience.

The pursuit of individuality is not merely a branch of evolutionary biology and survival sociology. It is, rather, the crucial subject matter of psychoanalytic psychology, to be studied in its own right, with its own terms, under its own conditions. Recall, here, James's classic statement, "When I say every thought is part of personal consciousness, 'personal consciousness' is one of the terms in question. Its meaning we know so long as no one asks us to define it, but to give an accurate account of it is the most difficult of philosophic tasks . . . The only states of consciousness that we naturally deal with are found in personal consciousnesses, minds, selves, concrete particular I's and you's . . . On these terms, the personal self rather than the thought might be treated as the immediate datum of psychology . . . No psychology, at any rate, can question the existence of personal selves. The worst a psychology can do is to so interpret the nature of these selves as to rob them of their worth."* Though he is ready, fifteen years later, to discard the notion of consciousness altogether, he never questions the existence of personal selves or so interprets them "as to rob them of their worth." Nor when he doubts whether consciousness exists as an entity and attempts that most difficult philosophic task of giving "an accurate account of it," does he deny the actuality of conscious functions in immediate and reflective experience. Yet it is from dealing with this sort of personal self that id and ego-interpersonal psychoanalysts backed away, finding shelter in biological and social perspectives. As background for the psychological model of shared experience, it suffices to cite this James view of personal self as the immediate datum of human psychology. His, moreover, is also the first modern psychology to treat consciousness as a continuous and flowing stream whose process and pattern are both immediate and reflective, and whose beginning, middle and end emanate from a personal self.

In the past decade of psychoanalytic discussion, the question Who am I? was often raised in terms of identity crisis, as though

*James, W.: *Principles of Psychology*. New York, Holt, 1890, vol. 1, pp. 225-226; italics omitted.

any effort to answer would shock the listener into a new dimension of existence. Usually raised with verve, directness and raptured search, it was supposed to be unanswerable within psychoanalytic metapsychologies. This obviously was not the case, since all ego-interpersonal psychoanalysts could quickly point to their public identities and credibly respond, I'm a doctor, a psychoanalyst, 180-18-2212. But the question was curiously posed and not actually put with the expectation of a response. Recalling the mood of that period, it is still difficult to be sure which side of experience was really being explored. The search seemed to be for a new frontier of sanity but at times also seemed to step over to the other side of that thin line.

Anyone asking Who am I? without immediate sense or awareness that it is his personal self alone — that is, his own I — who can answer is in serious psychological trouble. The question, in this form, is practically unanswerable in public terms because who anyone is, beyond his credentials of social and ego-interpersonal identity, belongs to the province of his own I as the only psychic source of individuality he possesses. To ask Who am I? as though someone else could answer indicates a discontinuity of the personal I from the social and ego-interpersonal me and some disturbance over the seemingly impossible task of reuniting them. But the question, ultimately, has no human answer. In Buber, for example, I and thou do not get together except in the theology of superhuman Thou.* So it is not a question in, for or about personal psychology even in its own terms; and it fails to elicit a sense of individuality as either human or natural.

Essentially, this question Who am I? reflects a deep discontinuity within basic categories of experience. It can be discussed and, I believe, just as well resolved in the language and thought of those who appear to be most concerned with the problem. Using Buber's terms, again, I and thou have dialogue and we have interhuman relations only within, never without, the medium of you and me. In active terms, I can meet your thou only through the mediation of my me, and thou canst meet my I

---

*Buber, M.: *I and Thou*. New York, Scribner, 1937, p. 75. This work, it should be noted, is poetic theology, not systematic psychology. I refer to it, however, as one of the best statements of this existentialist attitude.

only through the mediation of your you. Not I, in fact, but I-me can have dialogue with thou-you. These relations of I to me and thou to you are psychological. Now the distinction here of immediate from reflective experience clarifies why I never meet thou purely and simply without me meeting you, and why you never meet me purely and simply without I meeting thou. In ordinary psychological inquiry, the coexistence of I and me is rarely a problem; the two always appear in tandem, moving and changing, emerging and coalescing, integrating and reintegrating as a matter of course. In more specialized inquiry such as psycho-analysis, the problem is usually one of making room in the ego-interpersonal and reflective me for the personal and immediate I or in the ego-interpersonal and immediate me for the personal and reflective I; either way it is a matter of free and open interpenetration of the two.

In recent literature, metapsychology of psychoanalysis is usually dual or dialectical, emphasizing first I and then me, or the other way around. But in these dualisms and dialectics, one also usually overshadows the other. In keeping with the pop culture of mystical and existentialist doctrines, the pendulum, at present, seems to be swinging over into the transcendental realm. Instead of pitting the personal I in endless struggle against the social and ego-interpersonal me and against the biological and id not-me, while the pendulum rests here, psychoanalysis may attempt to study actual differences and probable relations among all three in a perspective with all three categories explicit — id or need satisfaction, ego defense and interpersonal security, individual psyche and its direction.

About the biological, social and ego-interpersonal perspectives, one critical question remains to be asked. If the patient undertakes psychoanalytic therapy already suffering distortions, disturbances and difficulties, why burden him with still another shell of attitudes and behaviors to cover them up? Deep-rooted as these problems are, how is it possible for him to adjust and adapt so that he can then act as though they did not exist? Or on what grounds, indeed, may he expect to do this within these perspectives? The answer, I propose, is to extend psychoanalytic perspectives to include a third category of individual psyche and its direction and extend psychoanalytic therapy from the id to the ego-interpersonal to shared experience. I return to this theme in Chapter 8 but, as background for it, present the structure of inquiry that makes such extension possible.

Chapter 7

STRUCTURE OF INQUIRY

As now demarcated, structure of psychoanalytic inquiry can support the third category of individuality – since established models are explicitly organized for the categories of id impulse and ego-interpersonal relation, and one major point of this structure is to distinguish metapsychology from psychology, it provides for all three, and others, at the (5) interpretive as distinct from the (1-2) empirical and (3-4) systematic orders. In Appendix A, Table I depicts this distinction. In its terms, it is now possible to disentangle the exploratory from the evaluative in psychoanalytic knowledge and outline three models of psychoanalytic therapy to cope with a special problem of its structure.

About many (1) observations and certain (2) definitions, it is true that if one psychoanalyst makes them, another working in his (5) perspective also can. And the same, of course, is also true about selected (3) postulates and (4) theory. Starting from the premise that psychoanalysis has intelligible unity, the notion of structure of inquiry covers this inner coherence of its body of knowledge, no matter who practices it. But what becomes of the many systems of beliefs, values and ideals by which each psychoanalyst and each patient, in his own individual way, interprets his experience as he lives it in therapy and elsewhere? The notion of model of therapy may be used to cover them, aligning id therapies with the biological model, ego-interpersonal therapies with the sociological model, therapies of shared experience with the psychological model.

Older ways of thinking and habits of practice are not the only obstacles to this distinction of structure of inquiry from model of therapy. Personal loyalties and group alliances in psychoanalysis, no less than in other fields, tend to be stronger than the empirical and systematic claims of the work itself. But the internal problems are also difficult, and many features still have to be further developed. In the recent past, these problems have revolved about separating essential from accidental features at each order of the structure, during each stage of the inquiry, for each experience of the therapy. There are some disagreements, I suppose, that no amount of argument and documentation can ever penetrate, but overall the structure is now firm in general approach and checked in basic outline.

In its view, the manipulation of psychoanalytic patients is a subspecies of the pursuit of certain beliefs, values and ideals of fifth-order metapsychology. It is therefore a subspecies of the interpretive question of which model of therapy is being applied in the actual working inquiry. In the biological model, for example, with its dominant emphasis on liberation of id strivings, the slant has to be more, rather than less, manipulative. This is as it should be because the psychoanalyst, of course, works for his patient to achieve this therapeutic objective. The same is true about the sociological model, as a second example, with respect to ego-interpersonal defense mechanisms and security operations. This is also as it should be because the psychoanalyst again works for his patient to achieve this therapeutic objective, even though the adaptation of defenses and securities is not as clear and uniform as the adjustment of genital primacy.

With the psychological model integrating the three categories of id impulse, ego-interpersonal relation and individual psyche, a psychoanalyst has alternatives to the manipulative posture. It becomes a matter of choice and he may therefore choose to do otherwise. He may decide that resolution of the therapeutic problem finally belongs to the patient himself as a matter of his own individual feeling, thinking and acting. In view of this basic freedom of choice, it is difficult to advance rigid formulas for any patricular psychoanalyst's participation in ordinary, everyday inquiry and experience with any particular patient, and it is impossible to itemize them in behavioral detail.

Prior to actual inquiry, all the psychoanalyst has is a general map of psychoanalytic structure to guide his use of his own experience with any particular patient. This means that practice of mature psychoanalysis, simply and directly, measures the maturity of that particular psychoanalyst. If he encourages and even uses his patient's distorted dependency in the attempt to liberate id impulse or mend ego-interpersonal relation, he may succeed in moving his patient toward his own preestablished objectives. But he must also remain aware that he, not his patient, is pointing the effort, so that the patient may then seek genuine individuality on his own without, in turn, triggering distorted expressions of authority that lead the psychoanalyst, paradoxically enough, into irrational submission to his patient. In such cases, pluralism in metapsychology provides, then, for the practically infinite individual differences among psychoanalysts and patients. Either the psychoanalyst or his patient may adopt any one or combination of id impulse, ego-interpersonal relation and individual psyche − in addition, of course, to the many others established or evolving in psychoanalysis − and still work together with the same structure of inquiry.

In addition to clinical empiricism, there is historical justification for this new approach, as well. Clearly evident in the biological model, of course, are traces of nineteenth-century philosophy and science, and they tend to persist in the sociological model. This philosophy and science look out at the study of human experience from behind a set of bifocals made up of dialectical and materialistic Marxism in one lens and biological and social Darwinism in the other. Their well-known focus is on the physical-material and biological and the social-institutional and economic to an inordinate degree and at the expense of the personal-psychological and spiritual. But notice that aside from their influence on psychoanalytic metapsychologies, these nineteenth-century themes continue to affect statements of theory of personality, especially its biosocial version, into the late 1940's.*

Against this background, the work of James and Freud acquires the significance of remarkable documents in their own time, especially the former's chapter on stream of thought† and the latter's on psychology of dreaming.** And they endure because in their unique ways, both explore dimensions of human psyche that

---

*Murphy, G.: *Personality*. New York, Harper, 1947.
†James, W.: *Principles of Psychology*. New York, Holt, 1890, vol. 1, Chapter 9.
**Freud, S.: *Interpretation of Dreams*. New York, Basic Books, 1956, Chapter 7.

are still major targets of major research efforts. If individual psyche were not so significant for personal fulfillment and psychic dimensions of uniqueness so significant for current psychoanalytic metapsychology — if, in other words, biology of impersonal id and sociology of interpersonal ego were the targets, instead — James's pioneering efforts would probably lose the high place they now hold in the esteem and effort of research psychologists and psychoanalysts. He, first and foremost, gives full recognition to the subjective, conscious and intuitive aspects of human psyche in addition to its objective, physiological and measurable aspects. Apart from later writings in logic and ethics that culminate in a pragmatic philosophy (of the two, I believe, his stream psychology will prove more durable), the giant 1890 psychology text still stands as a landmark of late nineteenth-century thought on the subjective, conscious and intuitive aspects of human psyche. Contrary to the trend of biological and social Darwinism then dominant, he simply and directly describes the terms and conditions of the personal self in psychology.

On the other hand, Freud builds far better than even he of all psychologists is aware. Fully accepting the biological and materialistic trends of his time, he undertakes the herculean task of setting a depth psychology of dreams and inner experience on the foundations of neurology and physiology. As currently seen, his route to this destination is indirect and circuitous, first supporting the widely shared rejection of empirical inquiry into human psyche and then attempting to base that very inquiry on the foundations of neurology and physiology that reject it. With this as its rationale, his biological model may be judged a failure — but a most productive and magnificent one, indeed. For though he finally cannot unify these disparate fields of inquiry, he boldly experiments with direct, two-personal inquiry, on one side supported by the work of Bernheim, Breuer and Charcot in hypnosis, cathartic therapy and psychopathology and on the other supporting such modifications of their work as the pressure procedure, free association, analysis of transference and conquest of resistance in id therapy, analysis of both transference and resistance in ego-interpersonal therapy, analysis of transference, and resistance and anxiety in therapy of shared experience.

There is, then, no need to choose between James and Freud. One's stream psychology supplements the other's psychology of unconscious experience. In this respect, they dovetail. Yet unlike James, Freud never develops his outlook into a coherent and openly stated philosophy of life, most probably because it does not fit into his efforts as natural scientist. In this respect, they differ. But consider the main point of this historical digression. Psychoanalysis originates in natural science and, breaking loose from its origins, becomes a human-natural science. In spite of the new application of theory of unconscious experience, neither id nor ego-interpersonal psychoanalysis takes its central vision for a thoroughly psychological therapy all the way. Hence the category of individual psyche and the new psychological model in order, finally, to cut the intellectual and scientific ties that bind it to nineteenth-century natural science.

The notion of structure of inquiry has the cutting edge for this purpose and, with increasing interest in its significance, has already demonstrated how sharp it can be. Three approaches already exist. They all first reorganize and refine the internal structure of psychoanalysis and then proceed to differentiate it from other psychotherapies. But each one reflects the special interest of its maker — a general psychological theory, a particular meta-psychology of human nature and development, the major terms and conditions of psychoanalytic inquiry and experience. The first maps a general psychoanalytic theory, from laboratory experiment to learning theory to developmental stages to awareness of change, and then sets it off from a special clinical psychoanalytic theory whose success or failure is not considered scientific and therefore cannot affect the general theory.* The second designs a grid, coordinating elements of psychoanalytic theory and therapy from the perspective of a special metapsychology without, however, making room for perspectives of other psychoanalysts or their patients.† The third outlines a structure that is directly clinical in origin and function, especially for the experience and inquiry both psychoanalyst and patient share, yet is also open to established as

*Rapaport, D.: *The Structure of Psychoanalytic Theory.* New York, International Universities, 1959.
†Bion, W.: *Elements of Psychoanalysis.* New York, Basic Books, 1963.

well as evolving metapsychologies.* I list these approaches not to compare them, since I have already done so elsewhere, but only to illustrate a variety of approaches the problem of structure stimulates in current psychoanalytic research. I turn, now, to a brief sketch of the third one.

Structure of inquiry guides the selection and treatment of terms and conditions that demarcate psychoanalysis. Its orders are as follows: (1) observation of gross experience, (2) definition of operational terms, (3) postulates of transformation, (4) theory of explanation, (5) perspectives on metapsychology. These orders are used to construct a bridge from (1) observations of psychological problems and (2) definitions of transference, resistance, anxiety and counteranxiety, counterresistance and countertransference to (3) postulates of genesis and function, structure and dynamism, and immediacy and reflection and (4) theory of unconscious experience — all worked through (5) perspectives on meta-psychology. (1) and (2) are empirical and practical, (3) and (4) are systematic and theoretical, while (5) is interpretive and specu-lative. (4) is the leading explanatory principle of all psychoanalytic inquiries and (1) through (5) set off experience of psychoanalytic therapy, as an integrated two-way effort, from experiences of other psychotherapies.

Following this outline of the structure, how does a psycho-analyst proceed? To put it schematically but not necessarily chronologically, first, he selects from detailed observations such processes and patterns of psychological problems as distorted perception, disturbed awareness and difficult living that his patient presents in the experiential field of therapy. Second, he introduces two clusters of definition, one about his patient's participation, the other about his own, in order to specify the distortions, disturbances and difficulties. Third, he adopts three pairs of postulates in order to transform the originally defined observa-tions. Fourth, he applies theory of unconscious experience to both the originally defined and later-transformed observations in order to explain one in terms of the other. And finally, he may interpret these psychological problems and resolutions, together with

---

*Wolstein, B.: *Theory of Psychoanalytic Therapy*. New York, Grune & Stratton, 1967.

almost any other aspect of life experience he and his patient find interesting, in accordance with one or several established and evolving perspectives on metapsychology. The first through the fourth orders guide procedures that psychoanalysts share by virtue of the experience they seek and explore with patients; the fifth embraces all systems of beliefs, values and ideals of all psycho-analysts and patients who undertake this inquiry to have this experience. In actual practice, both participants make the exploratory effort at each order from first to fifth.

The distinction of psychology from beliefs, values and ideals may be drawn for interdisciplinary purposes between (4) theory of unconscious experience and (5) perspectives on metapsychology, which makes it possible, in turn, to avoid the lifeless repetition of moralistic exercises in social and ego-interpersonal adaptation. Even apart from interdisciplinary purposes, it is clear that beliefs, values and ideals are present at every order of psychoanalytic structure and continuous in every phase of psychoanalytic experience. But the point of treating them as (5) metapsychology is to emphasize how essential it is to draw this distinction where the (1-2) empirical and (3-4) systematic meet the (5) interpretive and speculative. In no way does it imply, however, that psychoanalytic patients consider metapsychology less significant than psychology, only that they have to learn why these two sorts of judgment are not interchangeable and therefore cannot be reduced to one another.

Putting it in other terms, both the empirical (1) observation and (2) definition and the systematic (3) postulation and (4) theory are necessary for this structure of psychoanalysis. But they are not sufficient for its cognate experience of therapy, which also involves interpretive (5) metapsychology. Not for any reason of pure logic or scientific elegance, therefore, is metapsychology added to complete the structure. It is added for the factual reason that psychoanalysts and patients all have metapsychologies — more or less aware, more or less formal — that are present and continuous in their shared experiences because, simply, they themselves are.

But the fifth order in no sense substitutes for the first four, either. It is no news that perspectives on metapsychology, philosophies of life, slogans for action and metaphors of the ineffable that obviously affect psychoanalytic experience are not the essentials of psychoanalytic inquiry. Underlining the distinction of (1) observation through (4) theory from (5) metapsychology, however, may help to sharpen and evolve differences between inquiry and therapy in a new way. It means, for example, that only aspects of (1) observation that are specified by (2) definition may then be transformed by (3) postulation and explained by (4) theory, while other aspects of (1) observation that are interpretive and speculative belong to (5) metapsychology and set the working context in which inquiry takes form as therapy. I outline these orders in accordance with a perspective that affirms humanism, science and democracy in experience, knowledge and action in general and therefore also affirms individuality, truth and freedom for psychoanalytic therapy in particular.

The distinction of science from art may further illuminate this distinction of (1) observation through (4) theory from (5) metapsychology. Conduct of its inquiry is science, experience of its therapy, art. No matter how closely a psychoanalyst, as artist, follows the structure of his inquiry, the outcome of his efforts is in some unique ways the outcome, always, of his individual and induplicable psyche. As scientist, on the other hand, he seeks to demarcate the structure of his inquiry, refine its constituents and clarify their relations, in order to identify features common to the wide variety of experiences it shapes up. A psychoanalyst, then, surveys his field from the two points of view of science and art, inquiry and therapy, structure and experience. He finds gross experience in the therapeutic field a complex of observable processes and patterns in continual change. Under his selected terms of inquiry, he may find some recurrent and covariant (of these, some are genuine or distorted, others, vague or irrelevant). After frequently observing and defining them, as he tries to transform and explain them, he may make possible a whole new and unexpected series of observations of gross experience. He can do this because transformations and explanations, while related to each other, are also rooted in that field of experience he shares with his patient.

There are many other interesting relations of (1) observation and (2) definition to (3) postulation and (4) theory, but their discussion extends beyond this study. Consider, however, a major problem raised in all psychoanalytic inquiry, that is, to discover how therapeutic outcomes can satisfy requirements of the structure when there still is no reliable way of knowing in advance which observations are most relevant to which particular phase of the inquiry or even to any later application of the overall structure. This sort of question is usually best answered at later stages of the inquiry, but it is, of course, usually hard to know when the patient needs it for his own experience of therapy or his psychoanalyst's structure of inquiry. At present, it remains a matter of therapeutic art.

To summarize this brief sketch, the psychoanalyst treats selected psychological problems observed at (1), defined at (2), transformed at (3), explained at (4) and interpreted at (5). This structure is scientific by virtue of retaining empirical observation while producing systematic explanation. As a matter of methodological convenience, its terms may be symbolically represented. But psychoanalytic inquiry is not, then, purely symbolic or simply deductive. Theory (4) is linked to (2) definition through the mediation of (3) postulation; (3) postulation to (1) observation through the mediation of (2) definition; (5) metapsychology to all four through the mediation of beliefs, values and ideals of the actual coparticipants. No chain of systematic deduction is ever capable of demonstrating the existence of processes and patterns that at some point cannot also be empirically observed and defined. Even the most rigorous of systematic operations without empirical consequences, putting it briefly, fail to establish psychoanalytic knowledge about anything in particular beyond themselves.

Psychoanalysts are becoming more interested in their structure of inquiry. This growing interest is being nurtured by a variety of factors, and I now consider some that are both external and internal to the field itself. Psychoanalytic self-knowledge has always been a difficult and uncommon achievement that requires patient and intensive exploration, but two external factors threaten to make it more so. First, the insights of psychoanalytic inquiry are being widely and superficially applied with some success but without personal experience in many other psychotherapies, such as supportive, hypnotic, short-term, nondirective and drug therapies, in addition to group, milieu, family and community therapies. Second, established psychoanalytic metapsychologies are setting arbitrary limits to the psychological vision of patients who are less blocked than earlier id and later ego-interpersonal patients about sexual and adaptive functions; as observed in the psychological model, they suffer less from frustrated needs and social insecurities than from blockages in psychic freedom and self-direction.

These external factors alone, perhaps, might not motivate serious concern with the significance of psychoanalytic structure. But at present, psychoanalysts are also becoming more keenly aware of the limits and possibilities of a genuinely psychological inquiry and experience. To what extent is it biological as id psychoanalysts believe, or sociological as ego-interpersonal psychoanalysts believe, or even grammatical as the psycholinguistic analysts are beginning to teach? To what extent and, above all, in what ways do perspectives on metapsychology make psychological differences? In response, psychoanalysts are also turning to the study of factors internal to a psychological inquiry with psychotherapeutic objectives. In the course of exploring them, moreover, they are led to reconsider the nature of psychoanalysis as science.

Until the late 1940's, it was the custom to use metapsychologies as separate and self-enclosed systems. There were Freudians, Adlerians, Jungians, Rankians and so on, with each group hoping to keep the psychoanalytic experience entirely within its own special perspective. In their outlines, separatism in metapsychology far outweighs unity in psychology. They do not quarrel, for example, over whether anxiety is definable at the same order as transference and resistance, or over how transference, resistance and anxiety may converge with counteranxiety, counterresistance and countertransference in actual psychoanalytic experience and how – or even whether – these convergences are to be studied in process. Instead, they all engage in serious polemics about interpreting distortions in perception, disturbances in awareness and difficulties in living, and each group defends its own special metapsychology of instinctual dialectics, struggles for power, archetypes of the collective unconscious, conflicts of absolute will, and so on. As a result, they naturally see success in the patient's acceptance of their special interpretive slant and failure as their inability to trace it in his unconscious experience. But they follow out their own metaphors with very little regard for those of others, which, like the parallel lines of Euclidean geometry, are destined never to meet. Anyone who cares to cross them is branded maverick, his psychoanalytic therapy seriously prejudiced.

Among internal sources of this new significance of psycho-analytic structure, separatism in metapsychology is major. Most psychoanalysts, obviously, have positive outcomes in their therapeutic work without patients instantly and mysteriously converting to their special perspectives. But if something else is present here, what is that? Patients who make lasting and significant changes live and work through their psychological problems in the experiential field of therapy. From this it follows that a structure of inquiry actually governs the experience of therapy. In other words, this structure of inquiry uses its interpretive metapsychology in accordance with its empirical and systematic psychology in order to govern this experience of therapy. This does not mean that psychoanalytic psychology is or ever strives to be free and clear of metapsychology. Invariably, no therapeutic experience is whole and terminable unless the two move forward in tandem. But it does mean that no single perspective has exclusive and preeminent rights in the interpretive and speculative domain. And it also means that the three major psychoanalytic perspectives now established and evolving — biology of id impulse, sociology of ego-interpersonal relation and psychology of shared experience — may also be used in experiences of psychotherapy based on other structures of inquiry, and, no doubt, in problems in living anywhere else.

To be clear and become effective, psychoanalysis has to abandon the supremacy of metapsychology and put its structure of inquiry in the center of its experience of therapy. With open and radical pluralism in interpretation, it becomes possible to locate all established and evolving metapsychologies in the overall map of the field of psychoanalysis. And this pinpoints the stubborn fact that symbols of unconscious experience always have more than one interpretation. If there is a will, there is a way is still true about them because they are connotative rather than denotative and may be stretched to cover many different sorts of processes and patterns. Discriminating against none and hospitable to all, the experience of psychoanalytic therapy now belongs to those who undergo it without regard for their various meta-psychologies, and empirical and systematic orders of psycho-analytic inquiry now outline its explanatory range. And this pinpoints respect for everyman's right to make his own judgment of his beliefs, values and ideals. No psychoanalyst can accept less because no psychology of such judgment can, in itself, yield more.

All interpretations of unconscious experience follow from the interpreter's (psychoanalyst's or patient's) philosophy of ex-perience. They follow from his beliefs, values and ideals. It is true, historically, that only after disentangling the psychoanalytic experience from instinctual dialectics that other equally pro-grammatic perspectives could obtain a hearing. Many varieties now exist to choose from. Some are well-formulated, such as instinctual dialectics, struggle for power, collective unconscious, absolute will, and so on; others are less formal, such as the parapsychologies, existentialisms and mysticisms; a few are so individual and impressionistic as to resist institutionalization as school, movement or splinter group. But since the psychoanalyst's metapsychology is no longer dominant and the patient's acquires at least equal place, both inquiry and experience lose their former one-way simplicity. For no matter what beliefs, values and ideals a particular psychoanalyst happens to live, his patient may arrive at others that best accord with his own lived experience.

The new pluralism is especially relevant to the practice of psychoanalysis at our present stage of social history and cultural development. Consider briefly the wide gap between the pre-atomic and atomic generations, and little more needs to be said. Enforced by the new technologies, electronic communications, frontiers in outer space and exploding populations on earth, rising expectations in social, economic and cultural life, and by the urgency of unity on spaceship earth among all races, colors and creeds, this gap goes all the way down to the very deepest roots of our experience. Because these changes, however, are so rapid and without precedent, established systems of beliefs, values and ideals (and their symbols) no longer express the meanings they once did, while genuine new ones do not yet articulate the meanings of new personal experience. As already suggested, the main implication of all this for contemporary psychoanalysis is open and radical pluralism at the interpretive order of (5) metapsychology. Given this state of affairs, however, the distinguishing features of psychoanalytic experience are the constituents of its empirical orders of (1) observation and (2) definition and its systematic orders of (3) postulation and (4) theory.

From early beginnings in hypnosis and cathartic therapy, psychoanalysts have moved the development of this structure forward. They have stated and restated its definitions to simplify observation of deep problems in living; they have expanded and modified its postulates to guide transformation of defined observations, clarified and refined its theory to explain both the defined and the transformed observations in terms of unconscious impinging on conscious experience, all this under the umbrella of diverse metapsychologies. At present, they agree most about two clusters of (1) observation and (2) definition – transference, resistance, anxiety and counteranxiety, counterresistance, countertransference; about three pairs of (3) postulates – genesis and function, structure and dynamism, immediacy and reflection; and about the controlling (4) theory – unconscious experience. They disagree most, as already noted, about (5) metapsychologies that reflect individual commitments and color their statements of psychoanalytic psychology with all shades of beliefs, values and ideals. In the quest for innovation and in the heat of controversy, some even lose sight of its structure as inquiry and experience as therapy and use it to defend such extrapsychoanalytic ends as religious visions of man and utopian hopes for society, preferable codes of behavior and consensual environments of living, and absurdist doctrines of nothingness and arational mysticisms. Hence the new significance of psychoanalytic structure.

Psychoanalysis is here conceived as organized therapeutic inquiry into experiential fields of relatedness and communication.

The structure of this inquiry is designed for that special field of psychology that studies the operation of unconscious processes and patterns in personal experience. This structure essentially, I propose, sets the limits and possibilities of a special psychological therapy. For structure of inquiry clearly is not experience of therapy. It guides inquiry into selected aspects of gross experience, explaining psychological problems in living by defining and transforming them into conscious processes and patterns. Its (1) observations, (2) definitions, (3) postulates and (4) theory are not set forth apart from the (5) metapsychologies — impersonal, intrapersonal, interpersonal, transpersonal — which both psychoanalyst and patient bring to their common effort. And they apply this structure to a range of gross experience with the chief aim of expanding their scope of awareness.

Potentially, everything either coparticipant ever experiences of self and intimates, family and culture, and biology and society may be encountered in therapeutic inquiry, but in their common psychoanalytic effort, everything explored is in terms of the structure. For example, organic symptoms and disease may be observed during psychoanalytic inquiry but are directly studied in biochemistry and neurophysiology; definition and enactment of social roles may be observed but are directly studied in sociology and social psychology; judgments of beliefs, values and ideals may be observed but are directly studied in philosophy and ethics; cultural attitudes and general views of experience may be observed but are directly studied in anthropology and metaphysics. This present structure guides the psychoanalytic inquiry to the psychoanalytic experience, and distinctly so, by virtue of its special (1) observations and (2) definitions, (3) postulates and (4) theory.

The significance of the notion of psychoanalytic structure arises from deep and thorough changes in the conditions of psychoanalytic experience. Two external sources of change are the recent, rapid cultural and technological developments that create psychic pressures and possibilities unimagined in psychoanalysis in the early 1900's and the many new and flourishing psychotherapies using the insights but not the procedures of psychoanalysis. Two internal sources are the tradition of separatism among the many groups and schools whose differences are generally interpretive and speculative rather than empirical and systematic and the earlier absence of clearly stated foundations to put these differences into firm logical perspective. Of the three approaches to this significance of psychoanalytic structure already in existence, I outline the clinical one in detail. It integrates empirical, systematic and interpretive aspects of psychoanalysis into a structure that is both inclusive and coherent yet, at the same time, open to enlargement and extension in response to innovative therapeutic inquiry. Stressing pluralism and diversity in metapsychology, it has special significance, moreover, for the future development of psychoanalysis in new cultural environments.

Chapter 8

THE PSYCHOLOGICAL MODEL

Psychoanalysts are working toward a new structure of inquiry and experience of therapy that differ from those of the biological and sociological models and toward refinement and restatement of the basic outlines of psychoanalytic knowledge. Of all the psychological therapies undergoing change, today, psychoanalysis is probably in greatest ferment and undergoing the most fundamental changes. To see why this is so, consider the distinction of new knowledge from new technical applications, for it is useful in reviewing innovations in any psychological therapy. Transference, resistance, anxiety and counteranxiety, counterresistance, countertransference and their coordinated inquiry, for example, are innovations in psychoanalytic knowledge, while their intensive study in biological, sociological and psychological models of therapy or in psychoanalysis of individuals, groups, families and mass movements are special technical applications.

Anyone can distinguish knowledge from technique in accordance with his chosen perspective on philosophy of science, psychology in general or psychoanalysis in particular. I do not discuss that here, nor the difference between new knowledge and new applications of old, nor the notion of genuine novelty in knowledge or technique. I leave such fundamental questions to philosophers of science. All I mean to indicate is the self-evident proposition that a body of knowledge is not, literally, a set of techniques and that innovations in one are neither identified nor worked out in the same ways as innovations in the other. To illustrate this, take the difference between behaviorism as a program of theory and research, for example, and the varieties of behavior therapy designed to apply that program, adding new techniques of behavior modification, so far, rather than new basic knowledge of behavior. Consider further that it is also possible to apply a technique without knowing its rationale or know a rationale without applying its technique. In the internal development of any science, it is generally possible, then, to develop new knowledge without extending the technique or develop a new technique without extending knowledge.

There no longer is, and probably never again will be, only one model of psychoanalytic therapy. The biology of id impulse is no longer an either/or proposition (if, in fact, it ever was that), and perspectives and procedures are no longer excluded from the body of psychoanalytic knowledge on the ground, simply, that they are not consistent with that first model. This has been true, of course, at least since Reich, Anna Freud, Hartmann and Sullivan, among others, made their contributions to the sociology of ego-interpersonal relation. For after character analysis, ego psychology and interpersonal relation, it is fair to say that the biological model is in partial eclipse, to be used only in conjunction with the sociological model. Since the recent reconstruction of psychoanalysis as therapeutic inquiry in the individual and shared experience of its coparticipants, it is now also fair to say that the biological and sociological models are both in partial eclipse, to be used only in conjunction with the psychological model.

The distinction of knowledge from technique, furthermore, serves to contrast these three models by indicating how each one developed in response to its predecessors, because they all expand psychoanalytic knowledge. But the therapy of the two earlier models, using specialized techniques, no longer obtains full assent. Overemphasizing biology of adjustment, id therapy does not illuminate the study of unconscious experience without question. The arguments over libido and instinct theories are old and boring, and I shall not again review them here; I referred to some in Chapter 1. And second, the ego-interpersonal modification of this therapy, overemphasizing sociology of adaptation, also does not illuminate the study of unconscious experience without question. The arguments over ego defense and interpersonal securities are getting old and boring too, and I shall not review them here either; I referred to some in Chapter 3. Instead, I now contrast the two with the psychological model whose practice is gradually increasing.

Psychoanalysis of shared experience reflects deep and thorough changes in the structure of psychoanalytic knowledge. There no longer is any single dominant perspective from which to view the conduct of psychoanalytic inquiry, any single dominant interpretation within which to understand general human experience or specific psychological problems, any single dominant model according to which psychoanalysis stands or fall as structure of inquiry and experience of therapy. All this, now, is so well worked into leading principles that it is not about to be reversed in the immediate or proximate future. Not that psychoanalysts oppose interpretive metapsychology as such but rather that they oppose its use as the foundation of psychoanalysis. And not that they seek to reveal a deep and pervasive secret philosophy of human experience in the contemporary scene but rather that their major and distinct concern is a special type of inquiry, under special conditions, in accordance with special terms, for the special outcome of transforming unconscious into conscious experience.

It has, of course, always been true that psychoanalysts could choose from among many metapsychologies. At no time do Freud's instinctual dialectics ever dominate this field to the actual exclusion of all others. Besides his perspective, recall again Adler's struggle for power, Jung's collective unconscious, Rank's absolute will and so on, and how each once new and self-sufficient perspective entails its own new and self-sufficient procedure. But it is rather curious about this early period that innovations at any level — empirical, systematic, interpretive — usually lead to the formation of new and exclusive schools. Each innovator was, it seems, compelled to take a separate yet dogmatic view of the same orderly field of psychological inquiry. In this way, psychoanalysis itself very soon became a series of closed systems whose adherents — Freudian, Adlerian, Jungian, Rankian, and so on — could rarely probe their differences with one another. Interpretive metapsychology comes first, empirical and systematic inquiry, second; one is Freudian, Adlerian, Jungian, Rankian, and so on first, psychoanalytic therapist, second. But not any more.

The present situation exhibits indelible signs of change. Most obvious is that with unnoticed but increasing frequency, psychoanalysts tend to refer to themselves simply as psychoanalysts and only if asked then identify their perspectives on meta-psychology. Even though there always were more than one perspective in which to make interpretations, psychoanalysts could not always demarcate empirical and systematic orders to precede the interpretive order, as they now can, in the general structure of psychoanalysis. This is the historical point. Since empirical and systematic orders of present inquiry precede its interpretive order both logically and therapeutically, psychoanalysts no longer identify themselves by metapsychology because it no longer identifies their inquiry. Instead of splitting into a greater number of psychoanalytic schools, they tend to rely more on the fundamental unity of its underlying structure.

Creators of new metapsychology, on the other hand, no longer have to recreate the whole field of psychoanalysis in the image of their own terminologies. Nor do they have to recapitulate it as a special version of their separate system — nor, indeed, make it over as the framework of their particular innovations. The structure of psychoanalysis is now firm and well enough established, it is clear, to make room for new interpretive perspectives without being seriously dislocated at its empirical and systematic foundations. The (1) observations and (2) definitions, (3) postulates and (4) theory demarcating it from other structures of psychological inquiry are no longer shaken or displaced by new (5) metapsychology.

The recent rise and large turnover of existentialist perspectives illustrate this point well. They were first existentialist psychology and psychotherapy, then daseinanalysis and psychoanalysis, and finally existentialist philosophies of psychoanalysis and psychotherapy. In response to various existentialisms imported from Europe during the last twenty years, it again proved necessary to learn the hard difference between a process or pattern and its interpretation. Since the middle 1960's into the present, existentialisms are being used as philosophies, not whole systems, of psychotherapy. That is to say, one can practice any type of therapy — short-term, hypnotic, supportive and nondirective, as well as psychoanalytic — and still choose to be or not be existentialist in metapsychology.* It is now possible, simply put, to agree or disagree about issues in interpretive metapsychology and, at the same time, agree and disagree about issues in psychoanalytic inquiry. But it is no longer possible to draw a straight line from the terms, conditions and procedures of inquiry to the beliefs, values and ideals of metapsychology. In other words, a particular psychoanalyst may adopt existentialist or biological or sociological or psychological or other metapsychology and still pursue psychoanalytic inquiry.

Pluralism and diversity were not always so clearly established in psychoanalysis as they are today. When Freud, Adler, Jung, Rank and other early innovators first produced new perspectives for interpreting psychological disturbance, they declared them separate and independent. After segregating their groups and organizations, they engaged in much *ad hominem* argument and, of course, public psychoanalysis of their opposition. To defend their own systems, they criticized the others as limited and incomplete, even short-sighted and wrong-headed, or simply dismissed them as unpsychoanalytic and untherapeutic. Adlerians rejected Jungians; both rejected Rankians; and Freudians rejected them all. If it is not their type of therapy, it is not psychoanalysis.

In our current view of their self-enclosing acrimony and bitterness, it is not difficult to understand the reason for it. It is that their differences are essentially ideological and speculative, mostly philosophical and literally metapsychological. Recall that Freud roots psychological problems in conflicts between instinct and culture; Adler, in struggles for power; Jung, in archetypal manifestations of collective unconscious; Rank, in failures of absolute will. As though such wide variations in perspective did not express their intense singularity well enough, they further compound it by giving their different versions special names in the hope of gaining full possession of this newly developed field. One calls it psychoanalysis; another individual psychology; another analytic psychology; another will therapy. But in their innovative

---

*I discuss this further in my review of J. Bugenthal's *The Search for Authenticity* (New York, Holt, Rinehart & Winston, 1965); see *American Journal of Psychotherapy*, *20*:680-681, 1966. This book presents standard classical psychoanalytic procedure side by side with authentic existentialist metapsychology such that neither interferes with extended presentation of the other.

work, it should be noted, their different systems all hang from varied perspectives on metapsychology, instead of arising and being supported from the empirical and systematic side. They did it this way in order to put their differences front and center, for they sharply disagreed about interpreting what ails the suffering patient and what he has to make conscious in order to heal and become whole anew. They could not agree on the significant experiences and interpretations for psychoanalytic therapy and, around such disagreements, they separately systematized whole approaches to the whole field. But no matter what else they are, it is now clear, they are psychoanalysts by virtue of their common effort to seek clear awareness of some unconscious processes and patterns during therapeutic inquiry.

The situation is changing and as already noted, the signs are clear and distinct. Consider the recent and radical interest in psychoanalytic structure. It is, I believe, a first attempt to get at the root structure of psychoanalysis — not merely at beliefs, values and ideals about which psychoanalysts may agree or disagree among themselves and with patients but mainly at the relation of their metapsychologies to psychological processes and patterns (1) observed, (2) defined, (3) transformed and (4) explained. While the new approaches to this root structure may vary in detail, they all attempt to define, consolidate and extend the foundations of psychoanalysis. For even though any interpretive metapsychology is in some sense relevant to every psychological inquiry, regardless of where and when it is constructed and applied, no interpretation can displace the results of empirical and systematic inquiry. Psychoanalysis now focuses on intensive inquiry into processes and patterns specifically covered by theory of unconscious experience, as distinct from their metapsychology. And interpretive metapsychology, apart from this inquiry, no longer enjoys a special relation to the psychoanalytic structure.

This change has also brought about deeper changes in the psychological orientation of psychoanalysis. It may now be safely assumed, for example, that (1) observations of transference, resistance and anxiety, as well as counteranxiety, counterresistance and countertransference (2) defined during psychoanalytic inquiry also point up regular features of human experience in general; that this inquiry presupposes their statement as universally human; and that since human beings manifest them differently in various cultures under diverse (5) metapsychologies, whatever else being human does or could mean, it certainly requires the capacity to manifest them. Unlike such critical observations made and defined, however, a set of (3) postulates or points of view is simply adopted by the standard that they best guide transformation of defined observations for explanation, in turn, by (4) theory of unconscious experience — the basic and enduring theoretical construct of all psychoanalytic inquiry.

Consider briefly the four orders of (1) observation, (2) definition, (3) postulation and (4) theory. To this hard psychological core of psychoanalytic structure, then add the fifth order of (5) metapsychology, embracing all established and evolving perspectives that abide by certain standards of intelligibility, principles of logic and rules of procedure. Even a moment's glance at the structured relation of (1) observation through (4) theory of (5) metapsychology would suggest that no single system of beliefs, values and ideals is the single key to psychoanalytic experience. Psychoanalysts base their work, instead, on the overall structure whose inquiry results in special experience that, in turn, differentiates it from other psychotherapies. Since constituents of its five orders recur in every psychoanalysis done well, whatever else this psychotherapeutic experience involves, it is psychoanalytic to the extent that it involves these constituents of structured inquiry.

The significant thing about this structure of inquiry is its unreserved openness to practically infinite varieties of experience of therapy. Its terms make it possible for psychoanalysts and patients holding the most diverse perspectives to work together in mutual respect. The reason for this has already been discussed in Chapter 7. It is grounded in the basic distinction of (1) observation through (4) theory from (5) metapsychology that, within the structure of inquiry itself, supports efforts to demarcate empirical from systematic and both, in turn, from interpretive aspects of psychoanalytic judgment. But note that (4) unconscious experience is a construct of theory that explains, while (5) metapsychology is a perspective on beliefs, values and ideals that interprets.

The difference between explanation and interpretation is basic here, for it marks the claim of psychoanalysis to scientific discipline. It ordinarily enables psychoanalysts and patients who may disagree about major or minor beliefs, values and ideals to cooperate in exploring unconscious experience and still remain objective about their disagreements. Whether or not they hold the same metapsychology, that is, they can still cooperate in (1) observing and (2) defining, (3) transforming and (4) explaining certain psychological processes and patterns without at the same time (5) interpreting them in the same way with the same level of confidence. This difference has two other important consequences for the shape of psychoanalysis to come. It makes possible, first, the vision of a more harmonious community of psychoanalysts who, no less than with their patients, may also disagree among themselves about metapsychology and still cooperate in advancing the empirical and systematic structure of their inquiries. Second, it provides the basis for opening the structure to a new pluralism in metapsychology, whose importance is becoming more apparent with patients in transition from the more uniform biological and sociological to the more diverse psychological metaphors of experience. And the progressive development of models of therapy from biology of id impulse to sociology of ego-interpersonal relation to psychology of shared experience, of course, also reflects these changing beliefs, values and ideals.

It is in this way, then, that some psychoanalysts have attempted a constructive response to the democratic ethos of humanistic and scientific philosophies since World War II. Recent extensive practice of psychoanalytic therapy with patients raised in the new American frontier traditions, a well-educated generation of a very affluent society, has made even authoritarian-minded psychoanalysts develop a new sense of respect for the boundaries of each particular patient's psyche. Of the younger generation of psychoanalysts trained during this same period, moreover, some also could not follow and apply the rigidly oversimplified interpretive schemes of the biological and sociological models. These psychoanalysts, not unlike these patients, also inherit and try to live the same beliefs of humanism, values of science and ideals of democracy.

If all this is now so, the id or ego-interpersonal psychoanalyst may then ask what motivates this patient to seek psychoanalytic experience? The answer is self-knowledge. He seeks more and better knowledge of his available psychic resources outside his awareness in relation to those within it for making choices, clarifying judgments and sharpening decisions. The more a patient knows about his affective and cognitive resources, the more significance he may actually realize. And with it, he can change his life. Added to mere change, he becomes self-directing; to mere behavior, he acts toward ends-in-view; to mere communication, he commits himself; to mere relatedness, he is involved. No matter the preferred terms, there is a genuine difference between natural change and self-direction, behavior and action, communication and commitment, relatedness and involvement. Considering the first and second terms of this series, that difference comes down to the essential power he obtains through significant self-knowledge to transform his beliefs, values and ideals; indeed, to change his life.

In the present era of rapid change, furthermore, indefinitely extending the range of possible future experience, what psychoanalyst thinks he can still tell his patient what to feel, how to think, why to act? Especially since he faces the very same personal choices and decisions in his own experience, knowledge and action. Would he, if consulted, attempt to psychoanalyze President Nixon or President Johnson? Governor Wallace or General LeMay? Dr. Spock or Rap Brown? As therapist of psychological suffering, every psychoanalyst would hopefully make the effort, if no one else were available, to practice his psychoanalytic inquiry with any person in serious trouble, no matter who he is, where he lives, what he believes. And this is not the point. It is, rather, that psychoanalytic patients no longer suffer simply from maladjusted id needs according to the biological model or failed adaptations according to the sociological model. While patients now seem to make it in bed, at work and in society at large, they still have to make other far more radically personal choices and decisions that require genuine individuality — at least two generations away from problems of biological adjustment, at least one generation away from those of social and ego-interpersonal security.

Psychoanalysts since Freud and Sullivan, moreover, are confident about their therapeutic ability to deal with intimacies of the oedipus complex or the interpersonal scene of family romance. But it is no longer clear, with the traditional family coming apart, that all the family therapists trained in the next one hundred years will be able to return it to its prior state. Other sources and manifestations of social and cultural change are, of course, to be found outside the family structure, as well. Although study of their basic movements and directions is not directly within any psychological field of inquiry, it is nevertheless difficult to continue psychoanalyzing from day to day and act as though it were still the 1890's or even the 1930's.

While it may be argued that these changes are not yet crystallized into anything distinct enough to be called new culture, there is no doubt that something new is happening. It is a distinctly new mood made up of new perception, new thought, new action, which, if it continues to derive its meaning from the spontaneous here and now, the casual and experimental, the unexplored and unique, may well signal a more decisive break with the dominant id and ego-interpersonal satisfactions and securities than so far suggested. But without fundamental changes in psychoanalysis, those engaging in this new generation of culture will probably have to forego psychological inquiry into un-conscious experience governed by the psychoanalytic structure. They will have to go elsewhere because these new beginnings mark a decisive break with nineteenth-century pursuits of historicism, reductionism, materialism, authoritarianism and that one-sided rationalism based more in reflective than in immediate experience.

Still more important for psychoanalysis of shared experience, therefore reserved for special attention, is the new interest in both individuality and participation. To explore the psychology of shared experience, among other things, requires a genuine sense of individuality worlds apart from Freud's id ego and Sullivan's interpersonal self. The views of two such different psychoanalysts unexpectedly converge here because both follow the traditional lead of natural science. The reason they take the same negative view of personal uniqueness of human psyche may be found in the history and philosophy of sciences of man, since at least Darwin's 1859 *Origin of Species.* Some aspects of Darwin's influence on psychoanalysis and other human sciences were discussed in Chapter 5. Suffice it here to raise the methodological question of whether all structures of human science must follow the lead of natural science, such as, in this case, biology; or may psychoanalysis modify and extend that lead or even branch out and build its own?

In spite of enormous differences in their metapsychologies, the id ego and the interpersonal self bear this remarkable resemblance without regard for their intended use in a strictly psychological therapy. Since both terms approach the psyche from external points in its outside environment, they are, curiously enough, psychologically impoverished notions. Thin, dry, flat, the ego is so objectified and the self so depersonalized as to gloss over their most important feature of individuality, uniqueness or live sense, literally, of self-possession. Their common denominator, it is proposed, derives from assumptions about human psyche and its exploration that relate id therapy to biological and ego-interpersonal therapy to social Darwinism and to assumptions about evolution and development shared by other great nineteenth-century thinkers such as Hegel and Marx, Spencer and Huxley.

At the present time, patients do not present problems for therapy solely within the regular confines of either the biological or the sociological model. But id and ego-interpersonal psychoanalysts still use procedures and pursue goals that presuppose regular patterns of biological, social and ego-interpersonal behavior to which their patients try but cannot adjust and adapt, as though the new cultural changes were not relevant to the study of human psyche. The working inquiry in such fields of therapy, therefore, requires a patient's irrational dependency on his id psychoanalyst as father image or on his ego-interpersonal psychoanalyst as professional expert and guide who, working it all out, then points the way to adjustment and adaptation to the consensually expected environment.

But if, after id needs are satisfied and ego-interpersonal defenses secured, the patient still feels miserable, how does this therapeutic inquiry proceed? Since future alternatives of his ego-interpersonal environment are already incoming more diverse, less explicit and hardly expectable, how can this therapy even begin to work? In a word, it also changes. In their shared effort now, the patient does not ordinarily want his psychoanalyst to point out what he has to do, get him to understand why and show him how to go about it. With patterns of biological, social and ego-interpersonal behavior so much in flux, the range of his possible future, moreover, extends indeterminately outward and indefinitely inward. As one result of this, he does not easily surrender the direction of his life; nor, of course, does he easily surrender his own responsibilities for it.

Psychoanalytic study of shared experience, today, requires genuine individuality whose function is participation, genuine participation whose function is individuality. Because the id ego is too passive and the interpersonal self too detached, because a new kind of patient whose sense of self does not fit this passive or detached mood is seeking psychoanalysis with increasing frequency, because social and cultural changes are not yet over — at least for these reasons — it is necessary to keep psychoanalysis pluralistic at the order of (5) metapsychology; and for these reasons as well, it is possible to keep it available even to patients whose diverse metapsychologies are still in the process of being formed. This, in short, is the framework in which some psycho-analysts are now working toward a new structure of inquiry and experience of therapy.

The psychological model is part of the effort in this direction. In the shared study of shared experience, inquiry may focus more on the psychological and less on the metapsychological; psycho-analytic structure reflects this. Therapy may focus more on the exploratory and less on the didactic; psychoanalytic experience reflects this. And therapeutic inquiry may focus more on observation and inference and less on interpretation and specula-tion; to reflect this, the psychoanalytic focus moves from contents of beliefs, values and ideals to relations of conscious to un-conscious experience. On the distinction of exploratory psychology from didactic metapsychology, recall the earlier comments about the difference between explanation and interpretation. In accordance with it, the psychological model is designed to put these changes into effect. The psychoanalytic therapy it makes possible is more intensive and difficult because it is more immediate and personal; but its psychological outcome is also more reliable and enduring because it is more participated and individuated. Sought from the point of view of a rapidly and uniquely changing historical situation, this experience of therapy is now subject to even further ingoing participation and outgoing individuality.

In order to undertake this study of shared experience, a psychoanalyst has to know who he is and what he stands for. He may know his believed metapsychology without having to push it or apologize for it, and since he happens to hold that particular perspective rather than another, simply bring it into his experiential fields of therapy. He may do so without, of course, either becoming partisan about his own belief or turning deaf to another his patient holds but (hopefully, from my own point of view) remaining faithful to the belief in humanism, the value of science and the ideal of democracy. Beyond who he thinks he is and what he believes he stands for, however, his conscious and unconscious psychology is all there in that field of therapy, inevitably open and visible to his coparticipant in the inquiry. Sharply aware of the psychological challenge from unconscious experience, his own as well as his patient's, he enters into every psychoanalytic experience both encouraging his patient and preparing himself to study anything, any how or why. And after awareness expands to the limits of that particular shared experience, the patient may then also know who he thinks he is and what he believes he stands for, inevitably open and visible, as well, to his coparticipant in the inquiry.

Whether in the biological or the sociological model, it takes solid conviction to practice psychoanalytic therapy. In the third and current model, it takes conviction at least in similar measure. Even a brief glance at the wide gaps separating these major metapsychologies, from biology to sociology to psychology, would indicate this. There are still no irrefutable arguments in favor of any one perspective above the other two; about each, at present, there are many unanswerable questions. So long as arguments cannot be refuted and questions remain unanswered, these three models will continue to coexist. But even a brief look at the human psyche in all three, however, soon makes it clear that no special biological impulses determine it; no special social and ego-interpersonal patterns condition it; no special moral doctrines liberate it. From a strictly psychological point of view, nothing arbitrary or conventional ever attains privileged or transcendent status in ongoing, intensive psychoanalytic inquiry, which finally submits to the authority of human reason and syntaxic intelligence alone.

Putting it on a personal basis, I find great openness in the psychological model; I like the raw, tender and unprotected directness of this therapeutic experience; I seek a free sense of my own psyche experiencing my patient's sense of his so that we may both participate our affective and cognitive individualities in the shared psychoanalytic inquiry, usually curious in the search, sometimes pleased with the find, usually changing and moving about, sometimes stopping at points of review because one of us senses still further yet uncharted individuality of human psyche waiting to be explored. This psychoanalytic study of shared experience embraces efforts at their exploration in this field of inquiry.

Chapter 9

QUESTIONS ABOUT THERAPY OF
SHARED EXPERIENCE

P SYCHOANALYTIC inquiry, it is proposed, has developed from the biology of id impulse and sociology of ego-interpersonal relation to the psychology of shared experience. With this development, it is further proposed, manipulation and management of a patient's life may be reduced because the empirical and systematic inquiry itself, as described in Chapter 7, is no longer built around such attitudes. They do, of course, still persist, but only insofar as psychoanalyst and patient bring them into the experiential field of therapy. No longer inevitable effects of the psychoanalytic structure as such, they may be minimized, if not entirely eliminated. A firmer statement than this, however, is not possible, since the practice of psychoanalysis need have no better standards than the culture in which it is done, or can have more mature results than its coparticipants are actually capable of. A strictly psychoanalytic inquiry, then, does not get beyond the limits and possibilities of all other strictly psychological inquiries. To see the point where inquiry ends and interpretation begins, in any particular field, is to see behavior with others as distinct from experience of self, or a decision to adjust and adapt as distinct from a desire to explore and know.

Some potentialities of relatedness and communication are at present ordinarily impossible to obtain outside the field of psychoanalytic therapy. For it is and in some sense has to remain a peculiar sort of experience. When such potentialities, however, are ready for social and ego-interpersonal actualization, the problem loses its special psychoanalytic character; it becomes a problem of social and ego-interpersonal judgment outside the field of therapy. But some psychoanalysts and patients use the psychoanalytic experience in order to extend, rather than explore, their material and synthetic, aggressive and competitive patterns. Yet as long as any two particular coparticipants can undergo the experience so that their psychic individualities are revealed, this problem also loses its special psychoanalytic character; it becomes a problem of judging the social and ego-interpersonal origins of these patterns outside the field of therapy, again. The practice of psychoanalysis is ordinarily no better or worse, finally, than the culture in which it is done; its standards from day to day are no better or worse, finally, than those of its actual coparticipants. How can it be otherwise? If a culture highly esteems the manipulation and management of persons, why expect well-acculturated psychoanalysts and patients to do otherwise? If both are steeped in material and synthetic, aggressive and competitive values — which they do not, or, in fact, cannot, change — why expect them to make the psychoanalytic experience come out otherwise?

This third model of shared experience is essentially a psychological model of therapy. First, it focuses the inquiry by two persons on their common field of experience and awareness; second, it ranges as widely and deeply as any particular coparticipants require for intensive study of their distortions in perception, disturbances in awareness, difficulties in living; and third, it seeks to clarify pressures of social and ego-interpersonal identity colliding with personal and psychic demands for individuality. Since this model is essentially psychological, it is also comprehensive in that it is now possible to integrate it, appropriately modified, with its predecessors. Even after appropriate modification of all three, however, each one still only complements rather than displaces the others. In brief outline, genuine individuality and participation depend upon a logically prior system of stable ego-interpersonal securities, and stable ego-interpersonal securities depend upon a logically prior system of sustained id or need satisfactions. This telescopes psychoanalysis backward into its history, from the psychological through the sociological to the biological model, and it highlights the way psychoanalysis, over the years, has slowly matured through a sequential development of its major perspectives on metapsychology. This third psychological model, then, is comprehensive in that it accepts the integrity of inquiries and outcomes of its predecessors, while at the same time it sets the hard and valid psychological core of all three at the center of its present perspective.

Demarcating a comprehensive field of inquiry, this third model actually encompasses the environment of human psyche insofar as that environment has psychological significance. In this way, it is able to treat not only bodily need conflicting with social and ego-interpersonal identity but also such need and identity conflicting with individuality and self-direction. The difference between need and identity is probably self-evident without any more than a passing reference to the Freud-Darwin perspective of instinct biology – in its own right, already established as great tradition. In the aftermath of this evolutionary movement in nineteenth-century thought, it is now more important to consider instead the difference between identity and individuality. To do this briefly, it is necessary to indicate how they differ in one major respect. Identity is a function of socialization, individuality a function of personalization. Also note here the problem of loneliness so critical in the sociological model of ego-interpersonal relations. From this difference it appears, for example, that loneliness is a matter of social identity, aloneness a matter of psychic individuality, so that it is possible to be alone without being lonely, lonely without being alone. In other words, the individuated person can be alone because individuated, he is himself someone to be with and therefore need not be lonely. The painful fact of loneliness, in this view, derives from the unbalanced development of too much social and ego-interpersonal identity and not enough unique, personal individuality.

Certain difficulties in perspective and terminology clearly point up the need for this third model. Perhaps most obviously, these difficulties reflect a simple lack of adequate language and thought, which in itself suggests the extent of the failure of psychoanalytic psychology, so far, to realize its promise. Take the above attempt to state the difference between identity and individuality as the difference between socialization and personalization. Now, given the derivation of personalization from the Latin *persona*, meaning a player's mask or character acted, to call individuality a function of personalization does not begin to describe what actually happens in the process. While writing this aspect of difference between the two, I first thought of identity as social and individuality as psychic, but it is still not appropriate to adopt this usage and, parallel to socialization, speak of something like psychicization or psychization. These terms look and even sound a bit odd, I think, mainly because they cannot refine established usage in a climate of cultural opinion that does not regard the integrity of human psyche very highly. A term like psychicization or psychization seems preferable to indicate the process by which individuality comes into being; but I select personalization because its usage is general enough to connote psychic process that leads to individuality, without, however, the sense of tautology that individuation suggests.

As though to emphasize this low esteem for human psyche compared with the high esteem for society and culture, notice how often terms of socialization and acculturation are supposed to replace terms of the psyche in human science. For what process noun corresponds for psychic activities? The psyche, it appears, is not to have self-sufficient existence distinct from socialization and acculturation, while from the other side, socialization and acculturation are supposed to be self-sufficient without reference to individuating psychic resources, let alone their developmental significance. Of all sciences now devoted to the study of man, by virtue of its structure of inquiry, psychoanalysis is probably best able to study such processes and patterns and by virtue of its experience of therapy, probably best able to study their emergence and development live. The appeal of behaviorism as a program of theory and therapy, incidentally, is its avoidance of human psyche as distinct from biology, society or culture. This source of appeal, however, is its root defect as genuine psychology.

In both the history and the actual inquiry of psychoanalysis, the study of shared experience of individual psyche marks a significant advance. Its significance is that for the first time, a model of therapy available for regular practice does not manipulate toward any preinterpreted ends. In the nature of the case, individuality can no more be realized under principles of determinism and conditioning closely followed than it can be observed in outward behavioral performance closely followed. This, of course, does not mean that individuality is ever absolutely unconditioned; it obviously does mean that its critical conditions are inward and psychic and, finally, beyond the authority of anyone but its possessor. To the question, then, of whether psychoanalytic therapy is inherently manipulative, the answer is no, not necessarily so. It is manipulative, and only that, if consistently practiced without regard for the patient's and/or psychoanalyst's individual psyche and self-direction. It is not manipulative, and never that, if consistently practiced with regard for personal uniqueness, not just as interpretive metapsychology but essentially as psyche experienced.

In this way, psychoanalysis may follow the lead of experience of therapeutic inquiry as it finds it, automatic and repetitive but also creative and innovating; externally bound to the determinism of its environing biology or the conditioning of its environing sociology and ego interpersonality but also internally free to feel through and think over their personal import; capable of discrete responses to given stimuli in the individual's environment but also capable of integrative beliefs, values and ideals that can transform the individual and, through him, his environment. For this psychology of shared experience, clearly, the belief in individuality, the value of truth and the ideal of freedom are paramount metapsychology. A psychoanalytic philosophy, however, has yet to be written that emphasizes innovative to supplement repetitive aspects of mechanisms, dynamisms or patterns; that articulates their affective and cognitive as well as their determined and conditioned dimensions; and that indicates both limits and possibilities of the external, social and ego-interpersonal and the internal, psychic and personal relations.

In Chapter 8, I referred to the current social and cultural change. How, as presently manifested, does it affect the psychological model? It would be difficult to continue practicing id and ego-interpersonal psychoanalysis as though interpretive approaches to individual psyche were not also changing. Although id and ego-interpersonal perspectives differ in many significant ways, in respect to these very visible, ubiquitous social and cultural changes, they resemble one another. Their metapsychologies presuppose the very biological and social patterns of behavior already established, to which their patient tries but

cannot adjust and adapt. For this reason, their working therapeutic inquiry revolves about the assumption that he needs a
parental image or expert in ego-interpersonal relations, a professional partner or guide, to influence him to make necessary
adjustments for the promises of success and approval.

The contemporary patient, however, does not ordinarily require
his psychoanalyst to point out, while both are deeply into
psychoanalytic experience, what he has to do, get him to see why
or tell him how he has to go about it. Nor, if he really wants to
know his psychoanalyst's opinion, does he shy away from asking
about the environing expectations straight-out, so that it is no
longer best procedure to work over and around defenses and
security operations in order to exert a favorable influence. But
since established patterns of behavior are changing, the range and
variety of their future being indeterminate and therefore
indefinitely extended, he does not easily share responsibility for
these dimensions of his outward behavior and without the pressure
of influence, is usually ready to assume it.

In view of this, the id or ego-interpersonal psychoanalyst may
ask, What is this patient's objective in psychoanalytic experience?
The answer is self-knowledge. And why desire self-knowledge?
Because it empowers the freedom to choose and capacity to act
accordingly. But why prefer it to self-ignorance? Without getting
into the moral philosophy of this point (its dialectics touch large
issues dating back, at least, to Plato's *Republic*) suffice it to say
that knowledge is preferable because without it there is no way to
distinguish it from ignorance or to say anything about the
distinction. A patient seeks more and better knowledge about
himself, both within and beyond awareness, in order to coordinate
his available psychic resources with available environing conditions
for making choices and judgments, decisions and changes. The
more self-knowledge he has, the more significance he can have;
and significant self-knowledge transforms his life.

With social and cultural values changing, anxieties and counter-
anxieties are also changing. It is therefore especially important to
set straight this present psychoanalytic focus on psychic resources.
Psychoanalyst and patient are under new pressure to acknowledge
that conventional beliefs, values and ideals widely established as

patterns of behavior are not, therefore, beyond question. They must both be prepared to consider standards for acceptable perception and respectable action no longer in accord with inherited patterns of adjustment and adaptation. Perception has new modes; action, new environments. And the psychoanalyst is no longer expert in accommodating any special social philosophy, political ideology, cultural interest; instead, the psychological inquiry he seeks with his patient may range as widely and deeply as their shared use of theory of unconscious experience makes it possible for them to go together.

In this view of shared psychoanalytic experience, anxiety does not simply translate Freudian *angst* into English. Nor, of course, does counteranxiety simply extend it. For *angst* and anxiety, as used then and now, refer to two distinct sorts of experience, while counteranxiety is a recent addition to the psychoanalytic structure to indicate clinical observations that id and ego-interpersonal psychoanalysts do not make. But the difference between *angst* and anxiety is not limited to this empirical innovation of observing and defining counteranxiety. Nor, indeed, is it limited to treatment of anxiety and counteranxiety in the two clusters of transference, resistance, anxiety and counteranxiety, counterresistance and countertransference such that any one alerts the coparticipants to the possible existence of every other.

Still another fundamental factor, however, distinguishes the two. Freudian *angst,* generically, is dread that accompanies a sense of freedom in the midst of close adjustment and adaptation. It is a sometimes giddy, often dizzy sense of undergoing the primary distinction of the psychic from the social in actual, direct experience; it is that awful inner sense of being aware of something terribly amiss without, however, being aware of what that is; but it differs from fear in having subjective rather then objective stimulation. From this it follows, in short, that the ego-interpersonal self becomes anxious and insecure. Since it is the ego-interpersonal self that is essentially adaptive, when its patterns of relatedness are threatened and disrupted, this self again has to face vitally personal experiences it is no longer accustomed to facing and answering. Its original affective and cognitive resources, now in disuse, are not easy to transform for further integrative experience. But notice the unexpected paradox here that the adjusted and adapted suffer most from problems of angst and insecurity when, lonely, they undergo a dizziness of freedom to experience on their own; their adjustment and adaptation run into difficulties that both are, and in turn produce, the neurotic symptoms. As psychoanalytic perspectives change, however, and adaptation to the expectable ego-interpersonal environment is no longer a primary consensus in therapeutic inquiry, the clinical appearance of Freudian angst and ego-interpersonal insecurity may also be expected to change.

A definition of anxiety based on psychology as distinct from both biology and sociology is more appropriate for the shared experience of psychoanalytic therapy. Accordingly, this patient risks psychic failure every time he tries to make felt and known in patterns available for social adaptation the personal increment of any part of his funded experience, which, far from being passive and closed, is neither determined nor expectable. This, then, is what he becomes anxious about — the risks and responsibilities of his self-directive efforts that in success or failure, require modification of established patterning. Unlike the patient seeking biological adjustment, he does not find id impulses determining and overdetermining responses to his environment; and unlike the patient seeking social adaptation, he does not find ego-interpersonal patterns of his social and cultural environment rational or expectable.

But a psychological definition of anxiety also requires certain changes in established usage in the overall structure of psychoanalysis. Instead of applying the principle of psychic determinism in empirical operations, it becomes part of id metapsychology. Or instead of applying the adaptive point of view in systematic operations, it becomes part of ego-interpersonal metapsychology. In a pluralistic view, the acceptance of either notion is, moreover, a matter of preference in any particular experiential field of therapy; for neither is *sine qua non* in empirical and systematic inquiry. This is also true for the notion of available replacing that of expectable or consensual as the significant feature of the social and ego-interpersonal environment to which adaptation points. Since the validated environment is currently changing so rapidly, there is little ground to expect its consensus to remain expectable in the immediate and proximate future. It may, indeed, be consensually expected to continue to change at an even more accelerated pace. In future psychoanalytic metapsychology, as the environment becomes less a determinant or condition and more a field of experience, resources of individual psyche will acquire greater significance for its direction.

I want to mention a note, finally, about the relation of psychoanalysis to its available social environment. Among recent major sources of anxiety worth mentioning, for the adapted, maladapted and unadapted alike, is the new technological possibility that automation and computers can displace most industrial uses of human labor. But as this technology of material sufficiency for all men is sighted as a real possibility, the problem of sighting it psychologically and morally, as well, becomes critical. In response to this potential abundance, psychoanalysis is becoming increasingly concerned with deeper resources of human psyche once id needs are satisfied and secure — or at least envisioned as securely satisfiable. The current development of a psychological model of psychoanalysis is a useful coincidence, for its practice may help to bring about this incoming future of man liberated from Darwinist struggle for material survival and, as such, open out into vistas and dimensions of human psyche so far unimagined and unphilosophized. A reliable and productive structure of psychoanalytic inquiry, however, can serve this transitional process of loosening up the old and moving into the new. As suggested in Chapter 7, it can do this well because it is both coordinated and open — coordinated enough to align the significant terms of empirical and systematic inquiry; open enough to accommodate new visions of individuality, truth and freedom as metapsychology for that inquiry.

As a side effect of rising material aspirations, the question is often raised about justifying psychoanalysis in a world where so many still lack so much. In every first course in psychoanalysis, some student in good conscience usually raises it one way or another. Is psychoanalysis middle or upper-middle class science? My answer is no, for the following reason: pursuit of knowledge has always been compatible with — in fact, is necessary for —

healing the sick, feeding the hungry, freeing the enslaved, educating the young. This is indeed the only possible rationale for seeking truth, creating beauty, doing good, and being deeply involved with disciplines of science, aesthetics and morality in the face of widespread poverty, serious dislocations in culture and economics and irrational inhumanity of man to his fellow man. This, too, is the justification for pursuing psychoanalytic inquiry over extended periods of time with individual patients in the face of increasing pressures at clinics and hospitals for brief psychotherapeutic services. For without respect for knowing the true, appreciating the beautiful and celebrating the good, there can be no respect for the integrity of human psyche or, of course, for basic change in any kind of psychotherapy.

The distinction of psychology from metapsychology or awareness from responsibility, here, points up this new significance of individuality and self-direction in psychoanalytic therapy. And it focuses discussion on the psychological model, again. When the patient becomes responsible for his awarenesses, as he becomes aware of his responsibilities, if he does not sense and order his own individuality, it is difficult to see how he can proceed about his daily concerns in living. In a recent study, I develop this view.*

Reviewing that study, Dr. H. Guntrip questions the value of this distinction in therapy, instead describing the therapist as acting in place of parents to "supply, insofar as he can, those essential conditions of personality growth that the parents failed to supply."† He then criticizes me, quoting, " 'If the analyst participates to the full extent of his active powers of psychological inquiry . . . no matter how he then treats his patient, as one result of this division of labor, the patient treats himself therapeutically.' " Since, to him, "this extraordinary statement implies an addiction to belief in the omnipotence of science," he concludes that I do not grasp the implications of shared

---

*In *Theory of Psychoanalytic Therapy* (New York, Grune & Stratton, 1967, Chapter 5). For a statement in another context, see my contribution to the roundtable discussion, "Determinism and Freedom in Psychoanalysis," *(American Journal of Psychoanalysis, 28*:65-68, 1968).

†Guntrip, H.: Is psychoanalysis science? *Psychiatry & Social Science Review,* 2(4):26-30, 1968. The above and following quotations are from this source.

experience for therapy. This argument is a bit wide of the mark, and if it were not in the public record, I would not comment on it. In the first place, the "extraordinary statement" he attributes to me is so far removed from its original context as to misrepresent its actual meaning, which any objective reader who turns to pages 202-203 of that study can see.

But second, and more importantly, Dr. Guntrip fails to indicate a grasp of the notion that shared experience in any psychotherapy, because it is human, is continuously both affective and cognitive. For after he criticizes me for not having his metapsychology — "such attempts at rigid separation of scientific inquiry from metapsychology and strict limitation of therapeutic results to the operations of scientific inquiry," he asserts, "are unrealistic" — by the end of his discussion, it is he who holds this criticized metapsychology. Rigidly separating the two, it is he who insists on "new experience of fundamental ego-relatedness" that "belongs not to scientific inquiry but to real living," as though to imply that cognitive experience of scientific inquiry were itself not part of real living. But why does he think of separating the two? Psychoanalysis does not require this, which I try to indicate by placing metapsychology at the fifth order of its structure. No psychoanalyst would, in fact, seek this rigid separation of scientific inquiry from metapsychology except precisely in order to limit its use in the pursuit of therapeutic results, thereby limiting as well the operation of reason, cognition, intelligence, reflection, and in order, then, to make room for some special reality and experience that cannot withstand scientific scrutiny.

Consider further this theme of the relation of psychology to metapsychology because it depicts the fullest respect psycho-analyst and patient can have for each other's individual psyche. It does so without, however, implying that they relate as master and disciple, teacher and student, parent and child, owner and slave; or that the psychoanalyst should be, as Dr. Guntrip writes, "the kind of person who reliably supports his patient in such a way as to set him free and leave him free, by valuing him in his own right, to grow into his own individual selfhood." Without going into great detail, this view states, in effect, that a patient is valued in his own right to grow only if he does so under conditions his therapist sets for him, or that he becomes free only as his therapist sets him free, which suggests some distortion of the actualities of psychological freedom. For how, in fact, does a patient attain his own individuality and self-direction? Who, if not himself, can "grow into his own individual selfhood?" No therapist can, somehow, enter the core of his patient's psyche and do it for him in his stead, as though anyone could obtain his freedom from another without exercising it on his own, since no one not already free can ever simply be set free. If Dr. Guntrip still objects to my describing what he calls the patient's capacity "to grow into his own individual selfhood" as "the patient treats himself therapeutically," I would be inclined to agree on the ground that our respective psychoanalytic inquiries extend into different metapsychologies.

However, in mature practice of psychoanalysis, the field of inquiry has to be open at some point to the patient's own choice and direction. If there were no room for the free psyche in psychoanalytic therapy, patients would have to look elsewhere for it. This, especially, is the point of the third category of individuality. Working with the patient who is still troubled about satisfying id needs or has yet to make and defend his ego-interpersonal securities, a psychoanalyst using biological and sociological models may have to persuade and manipulate in order to exert favorable influence. But he proceeds this way because obviously no one else in that particular field — no other individuated person, that is — can do this for a patient whose relatedness is more distorted than real, whose communication is more parataxic than syntaxic. Even on this account, he need not, however, fixate himself in a persuasive and manipulative attitude. For in addition to his own sense and ordering of personal individuality, there is the patient's psychological potential for it. And this is the point where the manipulative and exploratory psychoanalysts part company, the former having to set his patient free, the latter working with a patient who has to set himself free.

Many patients, today, seem to know enough about existing patterns for satisfying needs and maintaining securities and are aware of how to use them. They have learned, more likely even overlearned, the correct needs to satisfy, the correct securities to maintain; they usually address the correct desires, plans and targets of behavior with the correct ways and means to think and feel and act. Choosing from among available alternatives, then, is not so much the problem as acquiring new ones. Some patients, of course, undertake psychoanalytic therapy in response to some tragic event or series of events that seems to throw their lives off balance beyond recovery; they seek therapy in order to balance out a new adjustment and adaptation. About such seriously disturbed patients, Sullivan expresses the following view: "So they patched up an imitation of normality — they stopped attempting to communicate the primitive material which is the essence of schizophrenia — whereupon the environment was no longer worried about them and everything went beautifully."* Notice his special phrasing of their effort — "they patched up an imitation of normality" — which is to say, these patients do not achieve even normal adjustment or adaptation once removed but only an imitation twice removed, from their inner psychic resources. The first removed would be a series of patterned normalities, the second is a patchwork imitation of it. But after they stop trying to communicate their inner experience that he terms "primitive material," the essence of schizophrenia suffered, it is true, but also the resources of individual psyche still possessed, they actually give up the struggle for personal sanity. In this sense, they are resigned, no longer seeing an inner thread of meaning and purpose and like blind sheep going through adaptive imitation of conventional normality.

But many psychoanalytic patients, at present, seem to adjust and adapt well enough for the twin pursuits of satisfaction and security. This is quite evident in the psychoanalysis of some ambulatory patients who, under pressure, may appear to become even more disturbed than hospitalized patients. Those well enough to obtain the standard satisfaction and security, meanwhile, present a different psychoanalytic experience — a new mood, perception, action and disturbance. Perhaps the difference for them, here, is really the difference between the 1930's and the 1960's, in part, the difference between great economic depression

---

*Sullivan, H.: *Clinical Studies in Psychiatry*. New York, Norton, 1956, p. 37.

and great social affluence. For they now complain about being anxious and miserable, empty and aimless, yet without much further use for the stereotypes and clichés they must adopt for material satisfaction and ego-interpersonal security. They master the conventional rhetoric well but, I propose, seek genuine individuality, a sense of personal uniqueness.

It is often observed that when individuality is false in fact, it may also work its way back into the outward personality and shake up already established patterns of satisfaction and security. As a clinical clue to this, false individuality usually appears more deeply disturbed than the actual conditions of life warrant; and it looks like a psychic hypochondriasis, a sort of interminable "psychoanalysitis" forever mulling over this or that id impulse and interminably reviewing this or that ego-interpersonal relation in search of still further refinements of satisfaction and security that are not about to become available. When the biological and social-materialistic biases of nineteenth-century science and philosophy are carried over into twentieth-century psychoanalysis, their myth and metaphor often reinforces the false belief that after biological needs are satisfied and social and ego-interpersonal defenses secured, all is right with the human psyche.

The choice of needs to be satisfied and securities to be defended, it is clear beyond doubt, stems from the arrangements and attitudes of established social, cultural and ego-interpersonal relations. Why, then, do they omit the individual psyche and its direction? They do now and, of course, will probably continue to do so until the social patterning of experience, both conscious and unconscious, expands to include this third category; that is, until the individual and unique can be coordinated with the biological and the ego-interpersonal in psychoanalysis of human psyche. But individuality is still a unique psychic quality. While in spontaneous action in the experiential field through which it is being lived, its very uniqueness makes its hard to recommend standard procedures that deal with it.

A lack of its secure sense, in addition, usually requires defenses against the anxieties and miseries that seeking it may evoke. This is the source of most fear and hesitation about its experience; the reason for calling it wierd, crazy, oddball and its possessor maverick, character, nut. After all, it is we, so the argument runs, who live the expectable life in the consensually validated environment; therefore, it is our view, not his, that must be right. But the value and validity of individuality is not subject to democratic ballot; on the contrary, a democratic ballot presupposes it. And since no expectable or consensually validated environment exists apart from those who already expect or validate it, the questions anyone seeking his own individuality has to answer are Expectable to whom? Validated by whom? Consensual for whom?

To set this category of individual psyche in the perspective of history of ideas, consider the interesting comparison to be made between seventeenth-century philosophy of science and our own, for its implications are still not fully drawn. In that great century of innovative thought, science of human nature was considered firmly established, while the structure, methods and results of the new natural science were judged shaky, confused and in need of clarification. Curiously enough from our current point of view, natural science had not yet become even the equal of human science, let alone its superior. Two illustrations here may suffice.

In the tradition of continental rationalism, Spinoza expressed full confidence in the belief that nature possesses eternal order, so that man may conceive human character based on "the knowledge of the union existing between the mind and the whole of nature."* In the second part of the *Ethics,* he states this union as "The order and connection of ideas is the same as the order and connection of things."† And in the fifth part, he describes the power of the intellect, "As thoughts and the ideas of things are arranged and connected in the mind, exactly so are the affections of the body or the images of things arranged and connected in the body."** For "an affect which is a passion ceases to be a passion as soon as we form a clear and distinct idea of it"††; and as corollary, "in proportion, then, as we know an affect better is it

---

*Spinoza, B.: *On the Improvement of the Understanding.* In J. Wild (Ed.): *Spinoza Selections.* New York, Scribner, 1930, p. 5.
†Proposition 7; above, page 149.
**Proposition 1; above, page 368.
††Proposition 3; above, page 369.

more within our control, and less does the mind suffer from it." The main point is that Spinoza has supreme faith that the final aim of man is to know the knowable *Deus sive Natura.*

And in the tradition of British empiricism, Locke emphasized the contrast between natural and moral science. "The commonwealth of learning is not at this time without master-builders," he begins his *Essay,* especially "the incomparable Mr. Newton," so that "it is ambition enough to be employed as an under-labourer in clearing the ground a little, and removing some of the rubbish that lies in the way of knowledge."* But when he considers "the idea of ourselves, as understanding, rational beings," he would place "morality amongst the sciences capable of demonstration: wherein I doubt not, but from self-evident propositions, by necessary consequences, as incontestable as those in mathematics, the measures of right and wrong must just be made out, to any one that will apply himself with the same kind of indifferency and attention to the one as he does to the other of these sciences."† His moral science, like Spinoza's, is also abstract and deductive, but again, it presupposes that science of human nature is a realizable venture.

Historically, this view of a moral and human-natural science later gave rise to eighteenth-century science of human nature, nineteenth-century science of society and twentieth-century science of human psyche. But the powerfully creative vision of Spinoza, Locke and others is not the point here; it is, rather, that they considered moral and human-natural science demonstrable without question, while they thought they had to clear "some of the rubbish that lies in the way of knowledge" from the new physics. In the light of this reversal of opinion over the last three hundred years, the significance of psychoanalysis for contemporary philosophy of science falls into special perspective as being part of a larger movement toward new science of human psyche.

---

*Locke, J.: *An Essay Concerning Human Understanding.* Oxford, Clarendon, 1924, p. 6; italics omitted.
†Above, page 277.

Chapter 10

THE PIVOTAL PROBLEM
OF SUGGESTION

IN outlining the models of psychoanalytic therapy, I have to this point emphasized some major sources of manipulation in metapsychology. All psychotherapies may, of course, be viewed as manipulative to the extent that they are practiced against a common backdrop of biological, social and ego-interpersonal Darwinism. In addition to the biological and sociological models, this in some ways applies to the psychological model, as well. It, too, inevitably exhibits manipulative elements until the patient reaches a sense of his own individuality and ability to use it — if only in response to the countertransference, counterresistance and counteranxiety he may observe during psychoanalytic inquiry. But manipulation in therapeutic experience is not simply a question of its extrapsychological sources, to be answered solely in terms of the biological, social and cultural perspectives of any particular psychoanalytic model.

Since breaking with hypnosis and cathartic therapy in the 1890's, practice of psychoanalytic therapy has undergone many important procedural changes, clearly but gradually expanding the field of psychoanalytic inquiry. First there was the pioneering observation and definition of transference, then transference turned resistance, then transference of ego defense mechanism or interpersonal security operation with or without libido theory, then anxiety in relation to both transference and resistance, then countertransference, counterresistance and counteranxiety converging with anxiety, resistance and transference — all these exemplify important changes in procedure not by any reasonable stretch of imagination derived from the cultural milieu of science and philosophy in which they were first stated. These are, essentially, internal developments of clinical psychoanalytic inquiry.

132

In each instance, the environing culture may perhaps have exerted external influence − in the most general sense, at least, that innovations in any structure of inquiry arise within one environing culture rather than another. But it is very awkward even to attempt the equation of external influences with internal innovations and practically impossible to succeed in the attempt. To put it under a hard light, consider that the first psychoanalytic procedure, itself clearly a radical force for freedom of the psyche, was actually developed in a monarchical culture, while on the other hand, adherence to its later modifications turned most strongly conservative and adaptive in a culture most proud of its democratic ideals. Although this puts the contrast in the extreme, which may make perfect sense to the historical dialectician, it suggests the point that equating influences with innovations is still a very awkward gesture made in the name of knowledge. As a matter of psychoanalytic structure, it is not possible to interchange the subject matter of psychology with its social and cultural metapsychology or reduce the one to the other.

In this view of the relation of psychology to metapsychology, consider certain aspects of the problem of suggestion. Its use occupies a pivotal position in the origins of psychoanalytic therapy in hypnosis and cathartic therapy. But it suffices, for this study, to begin with the 1915-1917 model of id therapy. The significant distinction is between direct and indirect suggestion; the former used in hypnosis, the latter in psychoanalysis. Though indirect, this newer usage is suggestion nonetheless; and in the shape of transference, it is the mainstay of this first model. Simply put, its focus shifts from confronting symptoms under hypnotic trance to studying their supportive conditions in genetic psychology and oedipal metapsychology. What, if anything, is wrong with suggestion? Generally speaking, nothing is or ever was. Parents and teachers, social and moral leaders, no less than hypnotherapists and psychoanalysts, have in some sense always relied on it, usually invoking the powerful support of reward and punishment, approval and disapproval and in the recent work of some psychiatrists and behavior therapists, even chemical agents and electrical devices. Anyone may make suggestions to anyone listening who, if responsible and self-directed, may then judge them on his own. So much for the ordinary standards of common sense.

In the first model, indirect suggestion is to be used in a very special clinical situation for a very complex purpose. Freud points it at two targets at once — new and still untested empirical operations and also certain beliefs about the metapsychology of early childhood. It should, however, be noted that persons with whom the id psychoanalyst uses suggestion and works out details of his metapsychology have already decided they are so severely disturbed as to need his consultation and as a result, on undertaking therapy, quickly make manifest their unconscious dependencies in plastic forms of transference. Especially in light of this — where unconscious dependencies are, clearly, natural and understandable — his use of indirect suggestion may be seen as working itself out in calculated, overbearing ways. For though he only indirectly aims it at neurotic symptoms, he very directly aims it at their underlying structure. The point of this procedure is that the patient, after genetic inquiry and id interpretation, learns to derive and interpret that underlying structure as oedipal childhood experience. When he can make another decision and take another course of action about it, his symptoms disappear.

In the *Introductory Lectures,* Freud does not leave this procedure to speculation. As long as transference is positive, he is quite explicit that "it clothes the physician with authority" and creates faith in his findings and views. In the absence of positive transference or when it turns negative, he continues, "the physician and his arguments would never even be listened to."* Here, as elsewhere in the last two of those lectures, he indicates the manner of authority positive transference confers on the psychoanalyst who then uses this transferred authority to support his arguments for the libidinal origins of neurotic symptoms. In most later critical work on the development of psychoanalysis, these 1915-1917 lectures provide important outlines of the id psychoanalysis of transference.

Even about this there is, however, some recent evidence for the traditional psychoanalytic style of reading back into earlier history some themes and meanings of later development, as though

---

*Freud, S.: *A General Introduction to Psychoanalysis.* Garden City, Garden City, 1943, p. 387.

Freud's writing could foreshadow all later perspectives and advances. One critic nicely writes himself into this retrospective fallacy, asserting that Freud calls for "strict equality between patient and doctor"* without discussing who, indeed, puts this strictness into effect. Following the *Introductory Lectures,* it is not at all clear that the Freud who calls for this "strict equality" is the same Freud who constructs the biological model. The quest for strict equality between psychoanalyst and patient is far more recent in origin, and its model of therapy is strictly psychic and human. Only since the radical study of transference, resistance and anxiety in relation to counteranxiety, counterresistance and countertransference in their field of actual occurrence, of course, does the notion of equality begin to acquire any real ground and substance in psychoanalytic inquiry and experience.

In the biological model, coparticipant equality would, it seems, be the last thing the id psychoanalyst thinks of. He is far more concerned about using positive transference to make interpretations stick and conquering resistance to their acceptance. To this end, he excludes from therapeutic inquiry and experience evidences of countertransference, hardly noticing counterresistance, not even mentioning counteranxiety. Working from behind this procedural wall, the id psychoanalyst directly precludes serious checking of his metapsychology in a dialogic way with the very person whose experience is being interpreted, namely the patient. He does not, then, have to seek a basis for distinguishing the genuine from the distorted in his interpretive perspective; nor, given the procedural wall, does he have to find the clinical basis for it in his patient's metapsychology. By his appeal to genesis, he can instead turn a patient's intuitions of his psyche back into the patient's own childhood experience, making indirect suggestion all the way. By the authority of his role in that therapeutic field, as enforced by his patient's positive transference, he focuses on developmental aspects of id impulse and leaves other significant aspects of his patient's personality outside their inquiry and experience.

Turning to the sociological model, the role of suggestion

---

*Erikson, E.: Letter to Gandhi. In *The New York Review of Books, 12*(2):12-22, 1969.

radically changes. In order to appreciate just how radically, it is only necessary to consider that the very language used to state the therapeutic action of psychoanalysis also changes in a remarkable way. In development of this model during the 1930's, the altogether unexpected absence of discussion of the psychology of suggestion, direct or indirect, has yet to be explored and understood. The ego-interpersonal psychoanalyst begins instead to discuss the role of therapeutic influence in securing and defending adjustment and adaptation; he deals with facilitating favorable change toward expectable, ego-interpersonal function. Even a long, hard look at the ego-interpersonal literature fails to reveal any intensive study of suggestion as a critical psychoanalytic problem, disappearing, it seems, as though by sleight of hand. It must be added that the central focus of this second major model actually differs from that of the first. Its central focus on autonomous ego functioning and consensual validation, rather, imply a critical attitude toward both suggestion and suggestibility. But though the therapeutic role of indirect suggestion disappears from ego-interpersonal discussion, it reappears unannounced under the new name of favorable influence. Termed this way, it retains an important therapeutic role.

In this connection, recall, however, that to the id psychoanalyst's mirror, the ego-interpersonal psychoanalyst adds the professional expert or partner who is also supposed to exclude evidence of countertransference and counterresistance from the field of therapy. This change in metaphor has distinct implications for therapeutic inquiry, extending ego-interpersonal psychoanalysis to previously overlooked varieties of defense mechanism and security operation. Openly acknowledging their emergence in the therapeutic experience, the psychoanalytic patient need no longer accept interpretation on faith in parental images or make a child transference to fit his psychoanalyst's metapsychology. For the first time, he has a clear right to possess and express his ego-interpersonal attitudes during psychoanalytic inquiry and in this changed procedure, may directly respond to his ego-interpersonal psychoanalyst's efforts to suggest or influence. With his ego-interpersonal self now fully in the field of therapy, he may feel and think about his psychoanalyst's psychology in evidence and, when he requires it, about the interpretations offered in understanding, as well. Above all, again for the first time, he may even offer his own.

This 1930's enlargement of the patient's field of active psychological inquiry, more than any other single factor, accounts for the steady decline of interest in distinguishing direct from indirect suggestion, a distinction so crucial for 1915-1917 id therapy. This does not mean that all psychoanalytic problems of suggestion are now resolved; it does mean, rather, that other more significant problems arise from enlarging the ego-interpersonal field of active psychological inquiry. In the face of newly defined ego defense or interpersonal security operation, attempts at indirect suggestion begin to look like deceptive efforts to hit the right interpretation and get a patient to accept and achieve the right ego-interpersonal adaptation. They may even deteriorate into circular interplays of defense and counterdefense between a psychoanalyst and the patient he is trying to influence in accordance with consensual conditions for social and cultural adaptation.

The ego-interpersonal psychoanalyst tends to become somewhat uncomfortable about this issue and, if at all, refers to the use of suggestion only sparingly. He devotes increasing therapeutic attention, however, to resistance and its relations to transference. As already noted in Chapter 3, this new ego-interpersonal interest, originating in revised ego metapsychology, eventually comes to dominate his therapeutic inquiry. Treating certain ego mechanisms and interpersonal operations as defenses for security and against anxiety, he does not yet offer a clinical definition of anxiety on a par with that of transference or resistance. By treating the anxiety itself as that which the patient defends and secures himself against, instead of exploring it through its own processes and antecedent conditions, the ego-interpersonal psychoanalyst cannot move his inquiry beyond it. Nor, finally, is he able to explore anxiety with a patient from within the unique perspective of his own personal metapsychology; not, certainly, in terms of his inner strivings for psychic freedom and self-direction. From the adaptive point of view, individual psyche and its uniqueness are outside his ego-interpersonal concerns — in the extreme, even delusional.

As a result, the problem of suggestion becomes increasingly difficult to approach coherently. Reacting against the authoritarian excesses of id therapy, the ego-interpersonal psychoanalyst does not use positive transference to gain support for his metapsychology. But he now addresses the open experience of anxiety in ways that add special strains to his already demanding work. He schools himself to accompany the patient's anxiety without, however, allowing evidence of counteranxiety to intrude. He had not, of course, formulated counteranxiety as part of the empirical inquiry, but if he had, he probably would have treated it the same as countertransference and counterresistance. No less than his id predecessor, he goes to great lengths to keep his personal psychology outside the therapeutic experience. Any shared interest in evidence of countertransference and counterresistance, let alone counteranxiety, he believes only deflects his patient's efforts from the main ego-interpersonal goal of consensual adaptation. He therefore participates only to observe and, as a general rule, counsels noninvolvement. But even in this role of participant observer, while working in such splendid detachment, he nevertheless seeks outcomes adaptive to the social order.

Lacking a clear distinction of psychology from metapsychology, it is, moreover, important to follow a precise procedure in order to exclude the psychoanalyst's personal psychology from direct experience during inquiry. If, in spite of this, he does show signs of countertransference, counterresistance and counteranxiety, he simply refuses to participate in their shared exploration, no matter how they actually affect his patient's effort at psychoanalytic inquiry. Since, according to the conventional wisdom, it is the patient who suffers the distortions, disturbances and difficulties requiring psychological attention, he obviously cannot be thought able to perceive and address his ego-interpersonal psychoanalyst who, as standard procedure, keeps his personality beyond the edges of shared awareness. If a particular patient then has such perceptions, this procedure puts him back on his own resources for checking how objective and genuine they are and in this passage, may make him think twice about his personal pecularities, funny feelings and messy thoughts — which his ego-interpersonal psychoanalyst does not engage for intensive inquiry because the peculiar feelings and thoughts happen to be about inadmissible countertransference, counterresistance and counteranxiety.

In adopting this attitude, the ego-interpersonal psychoanalyst may become confusing, even obscurantist to his patient. During therapeutic inquiry, he cannot openly clarify the difference between a problem in psychology requiring his participation and a problem in metapsychology for which it is optional. He puts the two together as equally beyond his involvement, arbitrarily treating the patient's experience of countertransference, counter-resistance and counteranxiety in terms of transference, resistance and anxiety, or simply barring it from the therapeutic field. A reductive approach at best, it pulls the rug out from under his professed participant observation that requires the one thing, interestingly enough, he is not prepared to do — pursue observation of himself participating in the actual field of his psycho-analytic inquiry. If he does not attend to his patient's observation of how he participates, and his patient then treats him to that old psychoanalytic joke about Who listens?, most often told about id and ego-interpersonal therapy, the story has a kernel of truth to it and the joke may be on him.

The ego-interpersonal psychoanalyst, of course, no more seeks manipulation as his conscious therapeutic objective than the id psychoanalyst seeks authoritarianism as his. Well-adapted to the adaptive point of view, he is usually committed to the political arrangements of democratic society. Even when not so well-adapted to his social and cultural environment, he at least gives lip-service to the democratic ideal, if only to acknowledge its predominance in the social milieu in which he practices his psychoanalytic art. Aside from adaptation to his society and culture, however, there is point to his method. It is his lasting merit that while avoiding definite involvement in alternatives that distress his patient, he is able to practice participant observation without actively compounding his patient's confusions with his own. His rationale is deceptively simple. So that a patient may better face his own confusions more directly, the psychoanalyst declares himself participant in the ego-interpersonal experience to observe but not be observed; somehow, at once being and not being present in that experience.

But the rationale also has a certain inner logic to it. Especially in anxiety, if only to stop the shaking of his ego-interpersonal foundations, a patient is unusually available to suggestive influence, more so, even, than in transference and resistance. Of this, the ego-interpersonal psychoanalyst is more keenly aware than the id psychoanalyst. In deep anxiety, a patient is most open to suggestion and influence, manipulation and management, as all brainwashers by now know only too well. More than anything else, he must have something to hold onto that shields him from the awesome, even terrifying qualities of a singularly shapeless experience without sensible beginning, middle or end. At that moment, he would limit its intensity and duration by almost any means put at his disposal by anyone claiming authority. So much for the anxiety.

Seldom noticed, rarely admitted, never explored, however, is the obscure and practically hidden factor in this ego-interpersonal experience — counteranxiety. As long as he may not consider and so far as he cannot know this about his psychoanalyst, it may be said that he also does not explore and know this about himself in that experiential field of therapy. As he does not explore the extent to which resolutions arrived at reflect his psychoanalyst's social and ego-interpersonal anxieties as distinct from his own, so he does not know the extent to which their respective anxieties are part of any particular resolution. It is primarily to preclude such inquiries, then, that the psychoanalyst not only avoids discussion of the problem of suggestibility in ego-interpersonal therapy; he even appears disinterested in the use of suggestion altogether, working mainly toward having favorable therapeutic influence.

In the psychological model, there is no such reluctance to consider the role of suggestion. The reasons for this divide off into the two major themes of the present study — structure of inquiry and experience of therapy. The major advance of this model over its predecessors is fundamentally the new significance of psychoanalytic structure. It is the hard and fast distinction, not separation in fact but distinction for inquiry, between psychology and metapsychology that cuts across psychoanalytic structure and for the first time, makes it possible to treat psychological processes and patterns (1) observed, (2) defined, (3) transformed and (4) explained without continual reference to their (5) interpretation. See Appendix A, again, for the arrangement of these five orders as Table I. By adopting pluralism and diversity in metapsychology, it becomes all the more important for each particular psychoanalyst to know his working preferences and commitments as clearly as he can. Now seeking both to share conduct of the inquiry and to individuate experience of the therapy, he may freely study any particular problem with a patient and, in so doing, set aside the therapeutic burden of using the patient's unpsychoanalyzed dependencies and unconscious suggestibilities. As a result of greater serenity about his own metapsychology, he may also work with greater lucidity in the psychoanalytic experience.

Where, as psychologist, does he inquire into how it is? As metapsychologist, where does he inquire into how it ought to be? Transference, resistance and anxiety define major observations of the psychoanalytic patient in the inquiry; counteranxiety, counterresistance and countertransference define major observations of the psychoanalytic therapist in that same inquiry. All six may be transformed by genesis and function, structure and dynamism, and immediacy and reflection. As defined and transformed, the original observations may then be explained in terms of unconscious experience. To this point, the inquiry is essentially psychological, both prior to and distinct from (5) interpreting or speculating about the (1) observations being (2) defined, (3) transformed and (4) explained. Hence the new solidity of psychoanalysis — it differentiates its orders of inquiry more clearly; it does not fit any individual's unconscious experience to any metapsychology before full exploration; and it accords no single metapsychology, psychoanalyst's or patient's, a priori supremacy. With psychology better distinguished from metapsychology, when questions of therapeutic significance are at stake, the psychoanalyst of shared experience can engage the full workings of therapy and, of course, attempt open study of the effects of his doing so.

In the psychological model, the role of suggestion no longer has to be carefully delineated as indirect in accordance with established id usage, and it also does not have to be replaced by the notion of influence in accordance with established ego-interpersonal usage. In therapy of shared experience, the psychoanalyst is prepared to acknowledge what he does as part of his individual participation. While deeply involved in inquiry and fully concentrated on its objectives, he may, for example, suggest syntaxic summaries of efforts and outcomes of inquiry to that point. The only authority he invokes here is that of syntaxic intelligence. If future inquiry fails to support any particular statement, it has no claim to further acceptance in that ex-periential field of therapy, except, of course, its parataxic and even prototaxic claims that shade his authorative statement off into authoritarian argument.

But under certain conditions, even the authority of syntaxic intelligence may appear manipulative, as well. Consider, for example, a psychoanalyst working to the point of emergence of his patient's psychological insight, yet also manipulating in the syntaxic sense of probing the adaptive ego-interpersonal facade of defense and security, searching hard for that individual kernel of insight and its induplicative effects on personal experience, hoping to observe that sense of individuality that leads to fulfillment; hoping because, in truth, nothing he can do ultimately makes it manifest; only the patient can make the sense and ordering of his own individual psyche observable and definable. Even the psychological model, in this circumstance, has to allow for manipulative elements until the patient reveals his affective and cognitive resources and develops his ability to use them. Then nothing any psychoanalyst can do, of course, manipulates any patient who knows now, perhaps for the first time, what it feels like to belong to himself and what it means to be his own psyche.

This psychoanalytic use of syntaxic suggestion, straight-forward and direct, for what it is, differentiates therapy of shared experience from both id and ego-interpersonal therapy. As already noted, the id psychoanalyst uses positive transference in order to manipulate a patient into accepting his biological metapsychology that liberates libido. He is, however, not concerned about reorganizing ego-interpersonal attitudes for this purpose, and his reliance on indirect suggestion reflects this lack of concern. The ego-interpersonal psychoanalyst, of course, also tries to influence his patient to accept his sociological metapsychology that in ego terms, liberates libido and adapts defense mechanisms or in interpersonal terms, satisfies needs and maintains security operations. Either way, psychoanalyst and patient adjust and adapt to consensual expectations of the particular environment in which they happen to be socialized and acculturated.

Neither id nor ego-interpersonal psychoanalyst, in any case, moves beyond indirect suggestion and favorable influence. Nor, indeed, does either move on to the deeply personal, original and fundamentally spontaneous sources of psychic freedom and self-direction. As described in Chapters 1 and 3, each in his own way fails to regard the rather simple proposition that only when human psyche is free can its individuality emerge. This cannot be overemphasized in any model of psychoanalytic therapy, since it takes a genuine sense of individuality, in fact, even to satisfy id needs and maintain ego-interpersonal securities reasonably well. A sense and order of individuality can heal the psyche – that is, make a person whole again. It is this healed psyche, this whole and integrated person alone, who can address the behavioral demands of biology and society, yet also seek the even deeper, perhaps more important, answers to these demands converging within the domain of his personal experience and beyond; who, in short, can relate affective and cognitive experience above all. And once he is aware of being capable of it, syntaxic suggestion checks out best.

Recalling the discussion of anxiety in Chapter 9, it may be useful to outline how the psychoanalyst of shared experience seeks to treat it directly. After first disentangling it from its metapsychology as speculated myth and metaphor, he introduces its observation and definition at the first two orders of psycho-analytic structure, adding immediacy and reflection at the third to coordinate its defined and transformed observations with theory of unconscious experience at the fourth. Anxiety is now as significant for empirical inquiry as transference and resistance. But the difference between the sociological and the psychological models, here, is not just a matter of extending the structure of inquiry. Guided by these new postulates of immediacy and reflection, it also involves a livelier mode of psychoanalytic inquiry and experience.

To put this another way, the ego-interpersonal psychoanalyst is distinctly interested in the foreground of defense mechanisms or security operations, and when he looks behind them to the anxieties, he, not unlike the id psychoanalyst, also finds id impulses and needs striving for satisfaction. The study and reshaping of this foreground of the therapeutic field, then, remains his chief and unique contribution. However, it is still true that this foreground is none other than past constellations of ego-interpersonal relations shaped and validated in their current social and cultural environment. On the other hand, the psychoanalyst of shared experience is also interested in this therapeutic fore-ground of ego-interpersonal attitudes but not primarily so; he looks beyond this outer envelope of personality through the glue of its anxiety into its affective and cognitive resources at the inner background of experiences. He is, of course, also interested in id needs pushing and pulling for awareness and satisfaction but again not primarily so; he seeks further psychological inquiry into still untouched potentiality and unrealized awareness of individual psyche, in order to hear the deeper personal beliefs, values and ideals his patient is so anxious about.

Following the five orders in structure of inquiry and pluralism in experience of therapy, a psychoanalyst may openly engage his patient in dialogic inquiry on the basis of syntaxic suggestion. Freedom to experience insight, the truth of open and structured inquiry, a sense of geniunely individual psyche – such are some scientific and humanistic aims of his psychological model. From the failed and fading aims of his predecessors, he may well learn the painful lesson of exaggerating aspirations for what is essentially a psychological inquiry. He does not have to absolutize his personal metapsychology or universalize its metaphors; he does not have to manipulate so that patients adapt to certain preestablished patterns. He is, instead, willing to exchange a narrower field of inquiry for clearer knowledge whose stronger foundations are set deeper within this narrowed field, an exchange that firmly, if unexpectedly, extends the scope of his psycho-analytic activities.

Graphically, the metaphor of a seesaw may be used to depict

the pivotal problem of suggestion in these three psychoanalytic therapies. It may also illumine the progressive line of development from biological to sociological to psychological perspectives. In the first model, therapeutic inquiry points toward the determinism of biological impulses — especially the libidinal, of course, in early childhood — and since the psychoanalytic problem is conceived primarily as uncovering that early domain of life experience, the seesaw most often takes the position of id psychoanalyst up and id patient down.

In the second model, therapeutic inquiry points toward the conditioning of ego-interpersonal defenses and social securities, especially the aggressive and assertive, of course, in social and cultural adaptation; and since the psychoanalytic problem is conceived primarily as readapting that adolescent domain of life experience, the seesaw most often takes the position of ego-interpersonal psychoanalyst up and middle and patient down and middle.

In the third model, both psychoanalyst and patient study relations of conscious to unconscious psychology of their particular field of inquiry and experience. Their therapeutic inquiry points toward the deeper range of individual affective and cognitive capacities for self-direction in their shared effort, and since the psychoanalytic problem is conceived primarily as exploring genuine individuality and personal perspectives to guide the reshaping of biological, social and ego-interpersonal processes and patterns in unique ways, the seesaw takes no one position more often than any other. It may move up, middle and down as psychoanalyst and patient sharing the inquiry and experience move it from either side, and it so continues until either or both achieve enough individuality, truth and freedom to get off.

Seriously practiced and well done, psychoanalysis may be seen as a uniquely self-defeating enterprise. This is not a paradox, however. Every psychoanalytic inquiry begins with a statement of problems whose resolution, as a general rule, indicates its natural end. The coparticipants work at it only until one or the other decides, in the above metaphor, to stop the seesaw — and both get off. The id psychoanalyst terminates when actual gains of daily life outweigh expectable gains of further psychoanalytic inquiry.

The ego-interpersonal psychoanalyst heavily relies on the environing social order for selection and judgment of therapeutic goals. From a psychological point of view, the patient is arbitrarily terminated in both models. For psychoanalyst and patient, here, are in the difficult position of having to base a psychological decision on such extra-psychological factors as instinctual adjustment and cultural adaptation. These factors, of course, fail to clarify the one goal of every psychoanalysis undertaken — that is, to terminate in terms of its original reason for being, namely the realized desire for greater self-knowledge. In the psychological model, it is, however, possible to consider termination the result of either or both participants seeing their inquiry and experience reach a natural terminus because nothing of psychoanalytic significance remains to be done. Given the personal psychologies and diverse metapsychologies of the particular psychoanalyst and patient involved, they reach a point of no further psychological responsibilities to each other.

Chapter 11

THE PSYCHE IN ANALYSIS

ONLY recently has it been recognized that becoming free of symptoms is not the same as changing psychologically. Patients today appear less inhibited about adjustive biological functions than early id patients and less insecure about adaptive social functions than later ego-interpersonal patients. They suffer far less from unsatisfied need and failed security than from blocked striving from freedom and fulfillment. It is not necessary to infer increasing id satisfaction and ego-interpersonal security from decreasing psychoanalytic study of them. It is, instead, possible to infer that id frustration and ego-interpersonal insecurity are transient symptoms that patients resolve without extensive reporting or, more simply, that psychoanalysts no longer treat the frustrated and insecure. I tend to discount these possible inferences and favor a third, namely that satisfaction and security no longer dominate problems in certain sectors of the culture at large as a result, among other things, of Freud's and Sullivan's classic findings on hysterias and obsessions now widely disseminated beyond psychopathology into child and educational psychology, sociology and political theory, art and literature and, in important ways, even into pop culture. Whatever the reason will turn out to be, however, the current clinical situation is still that psychoanalysts are more deeply involved than ever before in close study of the category of individual human psyche that includes and extends those of biological satisfaction and social and ego-interpersonal security. In this chapter, I relate this enlargement of psychoanalytic therapy to changing views of symptomatology.

In the last of his *Introductory Lectures,* Freud remarks that his therapeutic goal is to remove symptoms because that is what the patient seeks.* No matter what else it is to perceive symptoms, it is, of course, a profoundly social and cultural mode of communication, symbolization and legitimation. In light of this, any syndrome of events requires the cooperation of many other factors to become a symptom in conventional systems of beliefs, values and ideals. It is, in this sense, a social credential. As institute certification, for example, accredits a psychoanalyst's practice of this therapy, so the symptom accredits a patient's engagement in it. A perceived symptom, then, becomes a justifying condition — an initial condition, so to speak, that presents the patient's reason for seeking this therapy, that symbolizes the psychological problem he would resolve and that legitimates his intention to make the long-term effort.

There is obvious correlation between changing perception of symptoms and changing models of therapy. Without getting into the question of which changed first, it is possible, however, to put this correlation schematically. In id therapy, symptom perception is biological and instinctual; in ego-interpersonal therapy, it is social and cultural; in therapy of shared experience, it is individual psychological. It is probably clear, even from this, that certain symptoms legitimate the use of certain metapsychologies, and the same is true the other way around. In the early 1950's, some psychoanalysts not blindly attached to any single perspective for the entire field sensed this, no doubt, when they called one patient Freudian, another Adlerian, another Jungian, another Rankian, and so on. In this, they indirectly assert the close relation of perception of symptom, model of therapy and perspective on metapsychology. But they also set the major problem of research since then. With symptoms so variable, models so plastic, metapsychologies so diverse and pluralistic, the desire for order and solidity leads to serious interest in the basic features common to all distinctly psychoanalytic therapies. In Chapter 7, I reviewed the structure of psychoanalytic inquiry. Below, I refer to its significance for these changing perceptions of symptom, models of therapy and perspectives on metapsychology.

In this study, three models of therapy receive special attention

*Freud, S.: *A General Introduction to Psychoanalysis.* Garden City, Garden City, 1943, p. 395.

because they represent a clear sequence of development of interpretive perspectives from biology to sociology to psychology. As presented in Chapter 1, Freud's biological model from which Adler, Jung, Rank and others split theirs off is dominant until 1920. As presented in Chapter 3, the sociological model developed by Hartmann and Sullivan, among others, is dominant after 1940. But since the intensive clinical study of transference, resistance, anxiety and counteranxiety, counterresistance and counter-transference from the middle 1950's, as presented in Chapter 8, the psychological model is in the making. This listing, of course, does not mean that no others existed during the past seventy-five years. Nor does this historical sequence mean that earlier ones disappear after later ones appear. Variations, no doubt, always exist; others are and probably always will be practiced. But these are footnotes to a historical sketch of the three major models and some reasons for their construction.

It is not necessary, for this sketch, to review the history of the structure of psychoanalysis in great detail. It is necessary only to recall the major observations on which the major changes are based. There is, for example, the crucial observation that careful genetic study of affective trauma does not suffice to free psychological development in later troubled periods of life. If childhood trauma is not simply an affair of the id, since cognitive activity is in some sense present through all distortions, disturbance and difficulties, a psychoanalyst must treat his patient's experience as both affective and cognitive. This may, of course, look like a simple proposition whose truth is practically self-evident. But it had revolutionary implications for the biological model, and brought about irreversible changes in perspective and procedure. Putting the kernel of it in terms of id psychology, without the ego there neither is nor can be any study of the id.

With the patient's ego or interpersonal self now admitted into the field of therapy, something unexpected reshapes the psycho-analytic experience. Now that he can openly think about his id problems, it is but a short step to admitting their other aspects he thinks about, as well. In this expanding field of therapy, he begins to inquire into ego-interpersonal insecurities in addition to id frustrations. This change from biology of id impulse to sociology of ego-interpersonal relation, as already discussed in Chapter 3, is consolidated in new empirical emphasis on resistance and new interpretive emphasis on the adaptive point of view. All makers of the sociological model pursue adaptation to the average, consensually expected environment without actually establishing it as a matter of postulation. In psychoanalytic structure, adaptation is rightfully a principle of metapsychology and not a postulate or point of view; for it interprets rather than probes and, as such, has strong roots first in evolutionary biology and later in genetic sociology. In Appendix A, Table I depicts the difference between third-order postulates and fifth-order metapsychology.

The change from the biological and sociological to the psychological is a fresh effort. While id therapy works inward from psychic manifestations down into sources of impulse, and ego-interpersonal therapy works outward from psychic manifestations up into social and cultural patterns of adaptation, therapy of shared experience works with psychic manifestations where and when they are, to see how and what they can become, to decide whether and why they should be in the actual field of experience in which they can be (1) observed, (2) defined, (3) transformed, (4) explained and (5) interpreted. This third model is a fresh effort to psychoanalyze experience made up of psychological processes and patterns, occurring under psychological conditions and treatable in psychological terms, yet leaving interpretation of the beliefs, values and ideals carried by these processes and patterns, conditions and terms to the particular coparticipants involved.

The point is that psychoanalyst and patient are no longer locked into any one metapsychology or system of beliefs, values and ideals — Freudian, Adlerian, Jungian, Rankian and so on — simply by virtue of a shared decision to undertake shared inquiry into their shared experience. Nor, in fact, do they require prior commitment to any one special perspective in order to secure involvement in serious extended inquiry. Human relatedness and communication suffice for a factual account of the basic features of the experience. Inevitably relating and communicating, any two coparticipants have no choice but to experience each other and, in so doing, also have to explore and assimilate psychoanalysis of this experience in the only ways they alone can finally make it.

As background, recall some major observations guiding this gradual change. There is, for example, the crucial observation that transference does not take place in a psychological vacuum, to be psychoanalyzed by a mirror or expert as though he himself is not actively part of the very therapeutic experience in which he does it. This observation, indeed, proves to be the turning point. A psychoanalyst is now seen as a far more active coparticipant in the field of therapy than the mirror which reflects back only what is said to it, than the expert or partner who participates purely as observer with clear and detached eye or than the purveyer of any single olympian or sinaitic system of beliefs, values and ideals. Not only his learned psychoanalytic procedures but his persona, self and psyche actively participate in various therapeutic fields with great varieties of patient seeking psychoanalytic experience.

When it is later also observed that transference occurs in functional relation to both resistance and anxiety, it is but a short step to combining the two observations. Thus, if transference itself does not take place in a mirrored vacuum or with a detached expert, then neither does it do so as part of the cluster of transference, resistance and anxiety. From here, the third and present model of therapy of shared experience comes directly into view. For if the cluster of transference, resistance and anxiety is now also seen as studied from the psychoanalyst's standpoint, then it has to be studied in relation to the cluster of counteranxiety, counterresistance and countertransference. No less than the patient's psychology, it is now clear, the psychoanalyst's requires and deserves inquiry at least, if only in relation to his patient's during their long-term psychoanalytic experience together. How intensive it is or may become, finally, depends on the persona, self and psyche of both participants in a particular therapeutic inquiry.

Fundamental to the psychological model is this direct field approach to observation and definition of transference, resistance, anxiety and counteranxiety, counterresistance and counter-transference. Implicit in the gradual movement toward this new model, and equally important, is the demarcation of these six terms from perspectives on metapsychology. This developed in two significant historical phases. The first arose from the id psychoanalyst's inability to uncover original childhood trauma in each particular case. He began, instead, to find that he could not establish useful correlations between results of psychogenetic inquiry and objectives of current experience. As a result, his practice of psychoanalysis was increasingly threatened with becoming a psychology of pseudoevents in accordance with the particular id metapsychologist's ability to select and treat appropriate childhood fantasies as though they were also actual events. For this purpose, they imperceptibly assume the character of actual events because without their interpretive function, the whole exercise in psychogenetic study loses its logical meaning and therapeutic plausibility. In order to work well, it has to be supported by the patient's ability to find and document id metapsychology in his unconscious experience.

The second phase of this development arose from the ego-interpersonal psychoanalyst's inability to determine, for each particular case, the proper standards for adjusting id needs or adapting ego-interpersonal securities to current and future expectable environments. He began, instead, to find that he could not establish useful correlations between the adaptive point of view and social, cultural and ego-interpersonal alternatives of attitude and behavior. As a result, his practice of psychoanalysis was increasingly threatened with becoming a psychology of adjusting and adapting to vague standards of consensual expectation on the basis of limited knowledge. In order to work well, however, this procedure has to be supported by the patient's ability to see himself adjusting and adapting as both he and his psychoanalyst agree the society and culture really are, will be and ought to be. They both try to project ego-interpersonal bridges between these vague standards and what they can, at best, vaguely judge as the patient's best interests. Such ego-interpersonal bridges inevitably turn into social and cultural fictions because, without personal judgment of their psychological value, the whole exercise gets lost in search for external authority of adjustment and adaptation whose agency of approving and disapproving is largely diffuse and whose power to reward and punish largely impersonal and invisible.

The practice of both models, however, developed into a psychoanalytic study of shared experience on clinical grounds above all. In the biological model, the psychoanalyst's over-weening interest in genesis is checked by three hard clinical observations. First, patients are not ordinarily, in fact, sexually assaulted in childhood; second, they do not regularly report self-induced fantasies of parental assault, either; and third, after intensive psychogenetic inquiry, if they finally do make good the id metapsychology with appropriate history and fantasy, they still are somehow incapable of using this new knowledge for purposes of psychological change.

In the sociological model, the psychoanalyst's exaggerated interest in adaptation is checked by other equally hard clinical observations. First, patients do not ordinarily develop the ego-interpersonal self in order to deal with social and cultural problems but only act that way; second, when they do acquire any attitude or pattern as social and ego-interpersonal adaptation, it easily functions as a psychoanalyzed facade overlaying a deep and untouched psychopathology because it is not related in a systematic way to individual and unique personal psyche; and third, from the depressed 1930's to the affluent 1960's, this sociological model becomes increasingly estranged from realities of the very social, cultural and ego-interpersonal environment in which, curiously enough, it was originally superior in inter-pretation to the biological model.

Not unlike the undefined id impulses of the biological substrate, it is now clear, social and ego-interpersonal patterns of the culture at large are far more open and diverse — and far more fluid, ambiguous and multivalent, as well — than even the ego-interpersonal psychoanalyst ever thinks or teaches. For when patients are not sure which adaptations are in their own best interests, especially in love and at work, if they become too irrationally dependent and defensive toward their psychoanalyst to assume the personal risks and responsibilities for directing their own lives, they do not, then, accept oversimplified adaptive statements of what they should adjust to, and why, simply on their psychoanalyst's say-so. In neither the biological nor the sociological model, moreover, is any clear effort made to distinguish a structure of psychoanalytic knowledge from standards of prudence, negotiation and compromise that psychoanalyst and patient commonly use in their best interests.

It does not follow, of course, that turning to the study of shared experience resolves these inherited problems of id and ego-interpersonal therapy. A psychoanalyst is no better able to select just the right genetic or adaptive material for each particular patient as a matter of right procedure. Why, then, is there this third psychological model? The answer is the validity of psychoanalysis as body of knowledge, field of experience and structure of inquiry. The history of psychoanalysis could probably be rewritten, at present, from the point of view of these still unsolved problems. The day they are, both earlier models may be reworked with new confidence and practiced with new vigor. But that day is not near at hand.

In response to this situation, the psychological model takes a productive theory of unconscious experience as well as a working psychological procedure out of established metapsychologies deriving from premises and pointing to outcomes that cut off efforts at the empirical and systematic inquiry itself. This third model puts both the theory and the procedure on a more solid footing — theory governing structure of inquiry, procedure experience of therapy. Focusing on actual processes and patterns of the psychoanalytic field; defining clusters of transference, resistance, anxiety and counteranxiety, counterresistance, countertransference; transforming their genesis and function, structure and dynamism, immediacy and reflection; discovering when and how shared inquiry yields clarifying conscious material, when and how it locks in unconscious distortion — if psychoanalyst and patient succeed in their work toward reconstructing the distorted self, they will be far less concerned about readjusting to possible early sexual trauma or readapting to consensually expected environments. It is not at all clear, however, that a psychoanalytic patient is so well adjusted and adapted to such elements of biological, social and ego-interpersonal Darwinism that, uncouched and untutored, he would naturally select them on his own.

In my 1954 study of transference, certain difficulties with postulate transformation are discussed in both the biological and the sociological models,* though not yet in terms of postulates of

---

*Wolstein, Benjamin: *Transference,* 2nd ed. New York, Grune & Stratton, 1964, pp. 83-89.

inquiry or models of therapy. There, I trace Freud's use of genesis and compare it with Horney's use of function when one is used without being supplemented by the other. No matter what the therapeutic outcome of these one-sided usages is, their chief psychological outcome is still fallacy — essentially either genetic fallacy of equating the psychology of a process or pattern with its history or functional fallacy of equating the psychology of a process or pattern with its current operation. The best corrective to such one-sided efforts is, I still believe, not to conceive the source and meaning of the patient's problems in advance of actual inquiry, whether it is id impulse long-forgotten in the repressed past, or ego-interpersonal relation surfacing in the distorted and disturbed present, or psychological and located in the individual psyches undergoing shared experience. Close study of the actual problems becomes, rather, a matter of prolonged and intensive inquiry, moving back and forth across past and future through the present, applying postulates other than genesis and function (such as structure and dynamism, immediacy and reflection) without tightly tying psychoanalysis to the myth and metaphor of any one metapsychology.

But the important point is since neither genesis nor function is now dominant, it is no longer necessary to seek precise definition of the patient's problems at the very outset — or at any point prior, in fact, to the actual therapeutic inquiry. His private and particular problems, it is clear, are not yet knowable to either participant and therefore cannot be defined, much less resolved, until the later, even terminal, phases of the work. Defined with reasonable adequacy at the outset are presented symptoms that legitimate for him and rationalize for influential others, including his psychoanalyst, the difficult and painful undertaking of intensive psychoanalytic therapy over a long period of time.

Consider, now, the place of symptomatology in psychoanalysis from this point of view. With the gradual decline of interest in formation and perception of symptoms, since by definition, they are not basic psychological problems, the magical promise of psychoanalytic inquiry correspondingly declines. But notice that this magic of symptom removal first promised in the 1890's by hypnosis and cathartic therapy has, curiously enough, become the inheritance of behavior therapists who in the 1960's, promise it as the shamans of experimental and laboratory science. In psycho-analysis, dependence on the medical and behavioral models of symptom therapy, of course, proves illogical and impractical. Yet this original dependence may best account for the early promi-nence of the whole symptom industry. To become coparticipants in therapeutic inquiry, patients have to suffer and psychoanalysts have to diagnose and treat symptoms.

Perhaps the psychoanalysts who first opened and explored this new field of inquiry had to cover their interest in studying human psyche with the mask of a medical and behavioral therapy of nervous symptoms. And so they stated psychic function as somatic tautology, the notion of psychoneurosis itself, as stated and applied in psychoanalysis, being the best example of this confusing tendency. Following this course since the turn of the century, they actually produce a most exciting yet tangled chapter in the history of human sciences. This movement away from the biological and the sociological toward the psychological in psychoanalysis is fundamentally a movement away from medical and behavioral models of symptom therapy. Actually taking off this mask of nervous and somatic symptoms, taking it all off, reveals a field of dynamic psychology that is self-sufficient by its own terms, under its own conditions and in its own structure of inquiry. In a certain obvious metaphorical sense, it signifies removal of the symptom of self-doubt from the body of psychoanalysis.

Instead of genetic study of adjustment of childhood trauma in accordance with id impulse, and instead of functional study of adaptation to consensually expected environment in accordance with ego-interpersonal relation, another approach is under way. Psychoanalysts now look into the shared experience of the field of inquiry itself for significant observations of transference, resist-ance and anxiety. And they look to immediate contexts of that same shared experience, as well, for significant observations of counteranxiety, counterresistance and countertransference. This new psychoanalytic interest in the shared experience open to actual inquiry is essentially a psychological interest that may embrace any process or pattern of human psyche.

What, in this view, is human psyche? It is that field of processes and patterns, the relation of whose conscious and unconscious psychology is the major concern of psychoanalysts, who now try as directly as possible to do what the name of their discipline indicates — psychoanalyze human psyche. And what about this interest in shared experience? It represents the surrender of unproductive metapsychological certainties in favor of risks and responsibilities of more reliable psychological knowledge, insofar as such self-knowledge is available in psychoanalytic inquiry. This is not to write off (5) metapsychology as meaningless or even superfluous or write it out of the enduring concerns of psycho-analysis but, as change in emphasis, to shift the focus of inquiry from beliefs, values and ideals to empirical and systematic (1) observation, (2) definition, (3) postulation, (4) theory.

With this major shift, opening metapsychology to radical pluralism and diversity, psychoanalysts can first of all differ over some aspects of their beliefs, values and ideals and still work together in a common field of inquiry. At least equally important, second, particular psychoanalysts and patients can also differ over some aspects of their beliefs, values and ideals and still work together in a common field of experience. And third, this shift makes possible a psychoanalytic structure that does not rely solely on metapsychologies now in use — biological, sociological, psychological — nor require creation of still another structure every time a psychoanalyst happens to see a new slant on the philosophy of human problems and their resolutions. For the pursuit of any such metapsychology, as even the psychology of shared experience that I prefer, does not cause any logical or therapeutic difficulties. As long as the psychoanalytic structure itself rests on solid empirical and systematic foundations, a great many interpretive capstones may be added to it.

By making metapsychology a pluralistic and diverse order of inquiry, psychoanalysts do not have to create whole new models of therapy whenever they introduce new beliefs, values and ideals for that fifth order. Nor do they have to create whole new structures of inquiry whenever they introduce new empirical observations and definitions at the first and second orders or new systematic postulates and theories at the third and fourth. These various orders will probably change in the future as a result of making new (1) observation and (2) definition, (3) postulation and (4) theory, or as a result of extending any such constituents already established in the structure. But since this overall mapping of its foundations is firm and secure, it is no longer necessary for any single psychoanalyst to create the entire structure anew in outline or substance to accommodate new (5) metapsychology.

This psychological model, it is proposed, innovates clear directions in psychoanalytic therapy. Certain aspects of the work of many different psychoanalysts with many different patients may illustrate it. But neither the particular personalities nor their experiential fields of therapy, taken as illustrative, ever remain quite the same. While the statement of psychology of shared experience, for example, does not generally vary, observations of its therapeutic inquiry do, and infinitely so. For the making of each observation is a singular, individual and unique occurrence. Respect for individual uniqueness, in effect, is no more and no less than respect for the actualities of human psyche in their observed occurrence. It is clearly absurd for any structure of empirical and systematic inquiry — even, if not especially, psychoanalysis — to discard the notion of uniqueness altogether. To do so, curiously enough, first elevates the significance of interpretation in general far above that of observation in particular and in an undefined yet absolute way, then creates a structural lapse between the general and the particular. But it would indeed be very strange scientific knowledge whose empirical and systematic inquiry could not cut into its interpretive operations.

Among the many singular, individual and unique observations of particulars in psychoanalytic inquiry, certain new relations may be explored in accordance with the psychological model. Consider the following sample: First of all, the main focus of psycho-analytic inquiry is the actual psychoanalytic experience. Beyond all hearsay reports about remembered persons and events outside the experiential field of therapy — past, present, future — this shared field of experience is itself at once the source of observation, the support of inference, the guide to further inquiry and the measure of its interpretive metapsychology; in short, the subject matter.

Second, the order of metapsychology is pluralistic, diverse and open to serious interpretive differences without, however, imputing psychopathology to them on a priori grounds. From this it directly follows that when psychoanalyst and patient differ over matters of metapsychology, such differences also are not absolute indicators of psychopathology, even though they involve basic meanings of life itself and basic questions about how it may best be lived. It also follows that when a patient dissents from any beliefs, values and ideals of his immediate cultural environment, such dissent does not automatically indicate psychopathology, either. But there is more about this below.

Third, in accordance with this distinction of metapsychology from psychology, the psychoanalytic study of shared experience may become a more natural psychological enterprise by and for itself, with its own reason for being, its own purpose and its own end. After all is said and done, psychoanalysis is not experience undergone for the sake of something else, does not produce means to ends outside itself and cannot establish its subject matter in other experience. If psychoanalyst and patient are still persons and not things, then their shared experience cannot produce psychic means to extrapsychic ends but instead remains a means to its own end of expanding the scope of awareness.

Fourth, whatever else it does or may become, psychoanalysis studies human psyche. What is human psyche? It is all known capacities of feeling and thinking, desiring and willing, fearing and loving, hating and despairing, dreaming and realizing; in short, all known processes and patterns of experiencing. And how do psychoanalysts study it? Specifically, they study it under the ordinary and direct conditions of a two-person field of relatedness and communication; empirically, in terms of transference, resistance, anxiety and counteranxiety, counterresistance and countertransference; and systematically, in terms of genesis and function, structure and dynamism, immediacy and reflection, and of unconscious experience. In this way, the third model of psychoanalytic therapy becomes wholly psychological. Emphasizing experience rather than interpretation, it retains the empirical and systematic results of previous work without, however, being restricted to any one among the many metapsychologies now available. Regardless of whether psychoanalyst or patient supplies the larger part of it, any system of beliefs, values and ideals, formal ideology and pragmatic discipline or simply philosophy of life can provide the interpretive context of genuinely psycho-analytic inquiry, so long as it affirms belief in individual psyche, knowledge of truth and freedom in action. And this means fundamental respect for, among other things, the indefinite worth and integrity of individual human psyche, the logical and rational standards of scientific inquiry and the transformations of personal experience into new processes and patterns of attitude and behavior.

Fifth, psychoanalytic therapy is no longer a "headshrinking" operation, seeking above all to influence a patient to adapt to his social and cultural environment. Rather, it attempts a "psyche-expanding" experience to stretch his scope of awareness primarily, leaving adaptation to the available environment to his own best judgment. This change is long overdue because it is now often observed that by the time he is ready to adapt to requirements of the consensually expected, ego-interpersonal environment, these have also usually changed in some significant respect or other; which, incidentally, makes him appear wooden, stilted and mechanical in performing the ordinary tasks of daily life. Psychoanalytic therapy may be called a "psyche-expanding" experience, then, because this is what it does best as psychological discipline.

These are some significant relations now established in accordance with the psychological model. Even if there were no others, these alone would suffice to make it best suited for psychoanalyzing psychological problems. As background for this view, consider again the undeniable evidence that a clear and profound change, variously named transvaluation of values, counter culture and psychological revolution, is taking place in established systems of beliefs, values and ideals. Whether it is now in a transitional phase of a larger change not yet matured, or whether its own larger features are already firm enough to leave lasting imprints on the establishment to come are serious questions for both scientific inquiry and social criticism alike. While the conventional wisdom of the 1930's may not yet be dead, it appears, however, to be going fast; and this is plain to the public eye.

No psychoanalyst ordinarily deals with such questions, let alone tries to answer them, for they are not directly within his province. As an aware and sensitive participant, he cannot but respond, of course, to the mounting evidence for social, cultural and ego-interpersonal change in varieties of psychoanalytic experience. For some disturbed participants of our changing culture (refusing to adapt to things as they are, but still not able to say how things should be) still seem to find their way to psychoanalysis searching for greater self-knowledge and self-direction. As long as psychoanalytic metapsychology remains open and hospitable to diverse perspectives, they will probably continue to undertake psychoanalytic therapy. But they will dismiss psychoanalysis, and in my opinion, justly so, if they cannot even explore their own emergent points of view without, at every turn, bumping into the very social, cultural and ego-interpersonal conformities they are so deeply concerned about. If the distorted, disturbed and difficult of our dissenting culture then find it practically impossible to avail themselves of the healing resources of psychoanalysis, they are, on this account, right.

Patients who undertake psychoanalysis are generally self-directing enough in basic, if not always recognizable, ways and at some point, capable of psychological maturity. In this view, they undertake it, usually distorted about some disturbing and difficult anomolies of birth and biography from which, with expanding awareness, they try to free themselves in order to get on with other serious, more immediately personal concerns of living. Taking this view one step further, if in the biological model, psychoanalysts probe genesis so that patients adjust to accidents of birth and biology, or if in the sociological model they probe function so that patients adapt to accidents of biography and culture, they may effectively turn psychoanalysis into an instrument of the problem itself — inadvertantly, perhaps, but no less effectively. Why assume that patients should pursue any psychological inquiry that again confronts them with the very problems they are sick over and, in sum, simply expects to influence them to adjust and adapt? Why not assume, instead, that they undertake psychoanalysis in order to break through networks of id impulse and ego-interpersonal relation that bind them and, with increasing self-knowledge, break into new experiences based on expanded awareness?

No matter what public attitudes to this changing culture psychoanalysts may take as individual or professional group, it is important to distinguish such attitudes from their empirical and systematic inquiry. Open to pluralism and diversity in meta-psychology, their structure of inquiry neither admits nor requires their taking sides about this new culture. Nothing in the structure, as such, places psychoanalysis either for or against it. Guiding inquiry into certain generic aspects of human psyche, it does not empower psychoanalysts or patients to foreclose interpretation of these emerging beliefs, values and ideals. Interpreting them is not simply and strictly psychoanalytic, for they are not simply and strictly psychological. They are, instead, predominantly social in origin and cultural in function, moral in purpose and philosophic in ideal; they have to be if, indeed, they are to be resolved in these same predominantly social, cultural, moral and philosophic terms, as well. In this respect, structure of psychoanalytic inquiry is in full accord with the democratic view of everyman being finally responsible for the place he takes and the activities he undertakes in relations to his environment.

Appendix A

ANY effort to organize a body of knowledge encounters a fair degree of misunderstanding, and this structure of psychoanalysis is no exception. I alert the reader to two sorts of caution in order, hopefully, to anticipate two sources of misunderstanding. First, psychoanalytic therapy is not a mirror procedure in the sense that once and for all, it can lay bare a transcendental psyche free and clear of that therapeutic inquiry. No psychoanalyst can simply confront his patient with the promise to expose some essence that is and always has been simply there as pure self, personal ego or "onion" core — which may somehow reveal itself as though it were unrelated to that particular experiential field of therapy. Instead, this therapeutic inquiry is constitutive and reconstructive in the deeper sense of becoming itself a part of this new integrative experience of relatedness and communication, inevitably new because it has not taken place with anyone else in quite the same way before. This relation of inquiry and experience as means and ends is fundamental.

Second, this structure of inquiry has to be applied through the full range of its five orders for full psychoanalytic results. It is not possible to use it piecemeal — for example, lift a second-order definition out of the coordinated structure — and still obtain its full psychoanalytic application. Take the definition of transference that I state as follows:* when a patient introduces a significant change in relatedness and communication about his psychoanalyst, transference may be observed to be present, leaving to further exploration and analysis its genuine and distorted features. But this is only its second-order definition. It is necessary to work it through the rest of the structure, however, to obtain its full elaboration. For the definition of transference, this symbolic statement

$$t_n \cdot t \cdot G \quad F \cdot S \cdot D \cdot I \cdot R \cdot U \cdot [M_n]$$

represents the full range of its psychoanalysis. It may be directly

*In Wolstein, Benjamin: *Theory of Psychoanalytic Therapy*. New York, Grune & Stratton, 1967, p. 101.

Table I

STRUCTURE OF PSYCHOANALYSIS

Orders of Inquiry

Empirical		Systematic		Interpretive
Observation	*Definition*	*Postulation*	*Theory*	*Metapsychology*
(1)	(2)	(3)	(4)	(5)
transference t_n	transference t	genesis G	unconscious experience U	Freudian $[M_1]$
resistance r_n	resistance r	function F		Adlerian $[M_2]$
anxiety a_n	anxiety a	structure S		Jungian $[M_3]$
counter-anxiety ca_n	counter-anxiety ca	dynamism D		Rankian $[M_4]$ •
counter-resistance cr_n	counter-resistance cr	immediacy I		• • •
counter-transference ct_n	counter-transference ct	reflection R		• $[M_n]$

stated as (1) particular observations can be made of gross experience so that (2) they may be specified by the definition of transference, so that (3) they can be transformed by the postulates of genesis and function, structure and dynamism, immediacy and reflection, so that as both defined and transformed, (4) they can be explained by the theory of unconscious experience, and finally, so that in accordance with preferred perspectives on metapsychology, (5) they can be interpreted with the beliefs, values and ideals of the particular coparticipants.†

Other second-order definitions, resistance, *r;* anxiety, *a;* and counteranxiety, *ca;* counterresistance, *cr;* and countertransference,

---

*See previous footnote.

ct, may also be worked through these five orders of psychoanalytic structure, in a similar way, to cover their full range as inquiry and experience.

BIBLIOGRAPHY

Adler, A.: The Neurotic Constitution. New York, Moffet, Yard, 1917.

Bion, W.: Elements of Psychoanalysis. New York, Basic Books, 1963.

Bolles, R.: Theory of Motivation. New York, Harper & Row, 1967.

Buber, M.: I and Thou. New York, Scribner, 1937.

Bugenthal, J.: The Search for Authenticity. New York, Holt, Rinehart & Winston, 1966.

Darwin, C.: The Origin of Species. New York, Modern Library Giant, no date.

Dewey, J.: The Influence of Darwin on Philosophy. New York, Holt, 1910.

Dewey, J.: Theory of Valuation. Chicago, University of Chicago, 1939.

Dewey, J., and Tufts, J.: Ethics, 2nd ed. New York, Holt, 1932.

Erikson, E.: Letter to Gandhi. The New York Review of Books, 12(2):12-22, 1969.

Freud, A.: The Ego and the Mechanisms of Defense. New York, International Universities, 1946.

Freud, S.: Collected Papers. 5 volumes. London, Hogarth, 1924-1950.

Freud, S.: A General Introduction to Psychoanalysis. Garden City, Garden City, 1943.

Freud, S.: The Interpretation of Dreams. New York, Basic Books, 1956.

Freud, S.: New Introductory Lectures on Psychoanalysis. London, Hogarth, 1932.

Fromm, E.: Escape from Freedom. New York, Rinehart, 1941.

Guntrip, H.: Is psychoanalysis science? Psychiatry and Social Science Review, 2(4):26-30, 1968.

Hartmann, H.: Ego Psychology and the Problem of Adaptation. New York, International Universities, 1958.

Hofstadter, R.: Social Darwinism in American Thought. Philadelphia, University of Pennsylvania, 1944.

Horney, K.: The Neurotic Personality of Our Time. New York, Norton, 1937.

Jung, C.: Contributions to Analytic Psychology. New York, Harcourt, Brace, 1927.

James, W.: Principles of Psychology. 2 volumes. New York, Holt, 1890.

Jones, E.: The Life and Work of Sigmund Freud. 3 volumes. New York, Basic Books, 1957.

Locke, J.: An Essay Concerning Human Understanding. Oxford, Clarendon, 1924.

Murphy, G.: Personality. New York, Harper, 1947.

Rank, O.: Will Therapy, and Truth and Reality. New York, Knopf, 1945.

Rapaport, D.: The Structure of Psychoanalytic Theory. New York, International Universities, 1959.

Reich, W.: Character Analysis. New York, Orgone, 1945.

Schneider, H.: A History of American Philosophy. New York, Columbia University, 1946.

Sullivan, H.: Clinical Studies in Psychiatry. New York, Norton, 1956.

Sullivan, H.: Conceptions of Modern Psychiatry. Washington, W. A. White Psychiatric Foundation, 1947.

Thompson, C.: Psychoanalysis. New York, Hermitage, 1950.

Wann, T. (Ed.): Behaviorism and Phenomenology. Chicago, University of Chicago, 1964.

Wild, J. (Ed.): Spinoza Selections. New York, Scribner, 1930.

Wolstein, B.: Theory of Psychoanalytic Therapy. New York, Grune & Stratton, 1967.

Wolstein, B.: Transference, 2nd ed. New York, Grune & Stratton, 1964.

INDEX

A

Absolute will, 22, 49, 69, 97, 98, 104, 106
Adaptive point of view, 65, 139
as metapsychology, 149-150
Adler, A., 51, 69, 96, 104, 106, 148, 149
Adolescence, 30-31
Affective and cognitive individuality, 47, 110-111, 142
at background of experience, 144, ch. 6
Affluence, 80, 124, *see also* Metapsychology
Aggression and assertiveness, 44, 45
American culture, 62-63, *see also* Id therapy, Ego-interpersonal therapy, Therapy of shared experience
Analytic psychology, 106
Anxiety, 13, 49, 72, 164
as angst, 122-123
and counteranxiety, 121-122
as ego-interpersonal function, 39
in id therapy, 63-64
in shared experience, 143-144
see also Resistance, Transference
Ambiguity of Indefinite Commitment, 75-80
Atomic energy, 51, 54, 98
Authoritarianism, 111
and positive transference, 134-135
Authority of syntaxic intelligence, 142, *see also* Suggestion, as syntaxic
Automation, 54
Average, consensually expected environment, 40, 44, 47, *see also* Consensus
Awareness, 125-130
expanding its scope, 159-161

B

Behavior adjustment, 37
Behavior therapy, 50, 78-79
and symptom removal, 155-156
Behaviorism, 72, ch. 6
and behavior therapy, 102
and biology and sociology, 143
as hard-line behaviorism, 74-75
and human experience, 73-75
in theory of motivation, 72
Beliefs, *see* Metapsychology
Bernheim, H., 15, 90
Biological adjustment, vii, 62, 78
of id needs, 79, 152
and sexual trauma, 154, 156
Biological model, ch. 1, 22, 26-27, 32, 64
and nineteenth-century thought, 61-63, 89
highest development of, 21-22, 110, 147-148
its use of instinctual interpretation, 47
Biology and psychology, 9
Bion, W., 91
Birth control, 54
Birth trauma, 15
Bolles, R., 73
Breuer, J., 8, 9, 15, 18, 90
British empiricism, 131
Brown, R., 110
Buber, M., 84
Bugenthal, J., 106

C

Cathartic therapy, 3, 7, 8, 9, 15, 26, 76, 78, 90, 132
Character analysis, 23, 25, 63
Charcot, J., 15, 90
Childhood experience, 15-16, 19, 152